IDENTITY

IDENTITY

TRANSFORMING PERFORMANCE
THROUGH INTEGRATED
IDENTITY MANAGEMENT

Mark Rowden

GOWER

Published by
Gower Publishing Limited
Gower House
Croft Road
Aldershot
Hampshire GU11 3HR
England

Gower Publishing Company
Suite 420
101 Cherry Street
Burlington
VT 05401-4405
USA

Mark Rowden has asserted his right
under the Copyright, Designs and Patents Act 1988
to be identified as the author of this work.

British Library Cataloguing in Publication Data:
a catalogue record for this book is available
from the British Library.

ISBN 0 566 08618 2

Designed by Mark Rowden.
Printed in the UK by MPG Books Ltd., Bodmin, Cornwall.

Contents

Preface

This is a much-revised and extended edition of my first book, *The Art of Identity*, first published in 2001, and since translated into several languages worldwide.

Like the original edition, this is conceived as a book with a difference: it quotes no actual company names and displays no illustrations or graphics of any clearly identified existing identities or brands. Instead it focuses on the underlying principles that govern a powerful and therefore exceptional identity.

Readers familiar with the original book will find many additions that serve to demonstrate the integration of identity into the financial and commercial objectives of the organisation. This book is about defining your identity, whilst at the same time using it as an effective means of interrogating your entire operational strategy. In this respect it is about far more than identity alone. It is a unique process of improving and shaping all aspects of your operations through understanding your identity as you have never understood it before.

As a result you will be introduced to several new and radical techniques for creating and managing the entire presentational process of what you show, tell and do. Be aware that you will find no reiteration of or adherence to previous or 'standard' marketing theory. Those that seek performance must accept an above-average level of intent; an ambition and willingness that lesser rivals may view as extreme. Excellent and rewarding identity is indeed a form of extreme. It is beyond the norm; the extra mile of persistence and performance. If you are reading this preface then it can be assumed that you have an uncommon ambition for excellence and achievement. It marks you out as someone who seeks more and is prepared to put the effort into achieving that same. My point is that exceptional performance cannot be arrived at without equally exceptional levels of thought and action. You simply have to break the barrier of average; do that percentage more than the middle-runners. You need to push into the top ten per cent. Therefore it follows that becoming eligible for greater success means a willingness to probe the nature of current limitations – yours as well as the market you operate within. This means deviating from some of the more normal channels of thought, and striking out against the muddle and nonsense that identity and brand are so often portrayed as.

So, as a reader, you are offered much to think about within these pages. In this respect I make no apologies, for it is only through challenging present assumptions as well as taking the ambitious leader and their team beyond current boundaries of comfort that true progress can be achieved. I have seen this, been involved in this, many times. The reward for the effort is exhilarating. But it is effort. It is hard work.

The following chapters are positively intended to reorganise your viewpoint and operations. The entire idea is to prompt a change in values. Surface dressing is pretend change. Time and time again we see examples all around us where organisations superficially change their identity, whilst the same management with the same attitudes as before remain undisturbed. This book is proven to be much more. What you need is more profit. This means spending less and earning more, and at the same time doing it quickly. Speed is a permanent feature of modern life. It is as though we never have enough time and resources. Such a seemingly general comment, but yet for those unsure where to precisely concentrate their time and budgets it will eventually become the reason for their failure.

Whether we like it or not we all have an identity, and your identity will, even as you read this sentence, be an overhead. It costs money, even if it's just the sign above the shop. But, for the majority, this identity will not be earning its keep either. It may be an uncertain and misunderstood impediment to greater success, not the lithe and sprightly helper it most certainly should be. Worse, if the identity management is not completely integrated into the wider or more complete commercial strategy, as well as measurably understood by those leading the organisation, it can be a positive danger to survival. Identity kills. It should come with a warning. But is also your potential friend, giving birth to life and good fortune. How much better to turn the cycle of action to the positive and self-fulfilling direction of progress, and enjoy the rewards of an identity that with far less effort propels you towards your goals!

But enough of the preaching, for you have a book to read and delve into, and perhaps the last thing you want to read is a soapbox of a preface. It is you who needs to enquire and ask yourself these questions; draw your very own conclusions and list of actions. This book should be about you, and certainly not me. It is the process of finding what is unique for you.

Now I would like to say thank you, for in the writing of this book there have been a small but crucial number of able-minded friends who have, whether they fully know it or not, assisted the formulation of these words. They are: John Bundfuss, the financial SAS, if ever it were possible to have such a force, in particular for his conversational ruminations of 'above-average'; Andrew Dickinson, a most intelligent and sensitive expert in selling, since turned entrepreneur; Chris Heathcote, and his questful, zestful mind with regard to patterns and cycles; Jon Swaby, marketeer numero one; Irene Gil, gifted with an understanding of language, a bullshit detector more people within the 'branding' business would benefit from acquiring, and a penchant for magic dust; Mark Harrison, for furrowing my mind and leaving it more fertile; Suzie Duke, my trusted editor, with her sharp pencil and so perceptive way of making things always better; Denise Rowden for helping to manage a 20-year creative roller-coaster; Seth Rowden, for his exceptional clarity and far-reaching understanding of people and relationships; Oliver Rowden, for knowing how to bend the ball like Beckham and getting me to see beauty and skill in things I might otherwise have remained in ignorance about; and Bob Seymore, photographer since turned songwriter and musician, for his Texan courtesy, Tabasco and sheer kindness.

Photographs appear courtesy and copyright of AVEVA plc,
Stills Photography, Bob Seymore and Digital Vision.

Emotions

MANAGING ILLUSION

This book is about how to develop a powerful identity for your organisation and its products. You will learn a new perspective on building and then deeply integrating it into your overall operations. This goes beyond the status of the identity that is only the decorative add-on to the organisation or product it represents. You will gain a deeper understanding, and your identity will be a new vantage point from which you can explore your operational strategies as never before.

You need to be aware that many of the ideas within this book will challenge your existing thought patterns and are intended to impact on your organisational structure and commercial attitudes more deeply than previous understandings about the role of identity. This will form the basis of a new drive towards greater productivity and therefore profit. The interrogation of what is often mistakenly thought of as a 'black art' will result in your realising a greater sense of your true competitive advantages, a practical knowledge of the values that underpin

all identity is a lie, or is it?

your future success, and an improvement in the relationships and contributions of your internal and external creative people. In addition you will learn how to prioritise your marketing resources – in order to gain more output for less input – and in making these resources work smarter and harder you will learn how to rapidly measure their focus and quality so that all within the team can understand their purpose and desired effectiveness. The relationship between marketing and all other commercial operations within your organisation may, as a result of reading this book, never be the same. You will realise this with just a few, deceptively simple, compass bearings. The words in this book are intended to stimulate a valuable level of thought and debate within your team.

It is important to understand that whatever you currently believe about your identity, it is unlikely to be an accurate reflection of who you truly are. If you had no ambition, the quality and content of this identity and its portrayal of your organisation would be of little interest or consequence to you. However, it is assumed that you do have ambition, or you wouldn't be reading this book. By definition this means you have objectives already, or you are charged with the responsibility of defining some objectives. Before you begin to define these objectives you need to know one thing – that ultimately, all identity is a lie. That is not said to shock, but to ensure that you realise one critical point: identity is a mask you choose to wear; or it is a mask you choose to see. As such, it appears as a fixed image within an otherwise moving world.

This does not mean that a managed identity is necessarily untruthful. It is an acknowledgement that people and organisations are in a permanent state of change, and the image they wish to project may be at variance with the more exact truth of where they are today. Their image may be the intention of what they want to be or how they wish to be seen, rather than the reality of who they currently are. The point is that if the audience becomes aware that image and reality appear to be at odds with each other there is a 'reality gap', or words less polite. In terms of *your* identity, or the identity of your competitors, it is this deviation that represents a significant, and usually unaccounted for, profit or loss. To these ends this book gives you the knowledge that will help you to manage this commonly misunderstood and unfulfilled potential. In doing this it will show you how to create and then promote a set of deliberate messages that provide sufficient flexibility for your identity to grow as you intend. You will also learn to see clearly the links and integration that should bind your identity into your wider operational strategy, and why anything less than this is not only a waste of resources but an unnecessary step away from commercial success.

You are about to learn that there are identifiable laws regarding identity. These laws will give you, within the limits of your audience, a degree of control. You have a choice to match your identity to your objectives, and in doing so arrive more quickly and safely than if you leave these things to chance. In the process of achieving this aim you will realise that one of the most obvious benefits of a great identity is the opportunity it gives you to control how you are seen, and more than that, to be seen to be different. Your difference makes you visible and separates your personality from others. But difference alone is not enough. Your differential must attract, motivate and propel the instincts of those around you in accordance with your ambitions.

DEEP IMAGE OR DEEPLY MEANINGLESS?

Many organisations are content to believe that their logo, and little else, is their identity. Many individuals are also inclined to think it is their name (reputation) and nothing else that counts. However, both are shallow assumptions, for a logo or name, albeit often the most visible or verbalised elements of your identity, only signposts part of the whole truth. A compelling image is planned to succeed at all levels of communication: visual, verbal and behavioural. It is, in simple terms, what you 'show, tell and do'. Only then does an organisation or individual communicate an identity that builds success and starts to justify the money and other resources you are spending on it. Be aware that an unsuitable identity can only mislead its audience and obstruct the wearer, and that a complete lack of any planned identity produces worse: the unfocused and, inevitably, the unmanageable. Either way, your existing expenditure will be funding forward or backward movement. Good or bad, your marketing communications cost money to produce.

The more complete identity that we are concerned with here will cover all aspects of visual, written and spoken communication. To avoid the effects of chance, application and commitment are required. Achieving a successful identity, and reaping the rewards of having one, is not for the faint-hearted or fuzzy-minded, and clarity together with depth of vision is essential before you apply creativity. Your aim is to design without manipulation being either obvious or unscrupulous. If an identity represents opportunity, it also signals limitations: if we are to know who we are, we must equally know who we are not. Understanding your purpose and beliefs, then managing them with flair and dexterity, can be a private matter for an individual – a lone dancer controls his or her own movements. But the larger the organisation, the more difficult it is to maintain the choreography: a firmer grip on direction is required and, hence, it is important to focus the identity so it can be purposefully communicated and used to your advantage. It will also need continuous review, for all identity must ride the opportunities and traps of fashion and technology. Nothing, especially not your identity, can afford to stand still.

You need belief, and if you believe in yourself you should also believe in your identity. In addition, an appearance favourable to your aims and beliefs needs to represent more than surface alone. Presentation should permeate deep enough to convince, and then a safety margin of depth beyond. Think of this as 'deep image', where the surface of the identity seen is also seen to keep its promise. We can all think of manufacturers who have used the past beliefs and reputation of a badge or marque on a new but inferior product. When the truth is realised, the customer (and staff) feel cheated. Once cheated, the customer's memory of dissatisfaction persists for a considerable time, if not forever.

Identifying your core beliefs is no easy matter – or rather it is when you begin to realise that you arrive at your beliefs and values by first concentrating on your differential, a process we will return to later; but for many, unaware of exactly how best to proceed, the task seems daunting and it is a fact that most individuals and management teams fail before they start. If you ask the majority of organisations to describe their values, it is interesting to note that few can offer any clear or profitable answers. But you must, for if you don't know, how can you expect your market to know? Simply insist on knowing who you are and where you are going, by setting values and desired outcomes. Failure to identify these beliefs produces an unpredictability which, in turn, will inevitably produce a shortfall in understanding and communication. This failure can easily germinate throughout service, product design, manufacture and personnel, finally impacting upon the entire venture and its level of profit or loss. It is not just customers who quickly discover the limitations of an identity, it is staff too.

it is a fact that business is far less logical than most of us presume

To become successful, a team must share the same standards and values. They will feel energised in the knowledge that their contribution to the whole, whether major or minor, knowingly fits within the aims and beliefs of the overall venture. As a result they will communicate these shared beliefs as one. In this respect, a smaller organisation, or cell, has an advantage over a larger one when it comes to punching beyond its weight. A vision is more easily shared and can therefore become so much more powerful within a smaller team.

Your beliefs need to communicate themselves to your audience without confusing them. As well as ensuring clarity, all good interpretation requires an allowance for others' emotions. You need to communicate often with those who have no intention of communicating with you. So do you mislead, repel or attract them? If you attract or repel, will it be for the correct reasons? Do not answer these questions too hastily for there will be times when you will need to do both. Just one example of this is recruitment advertising, where you must filter potential applicants into action and inaction. You certainly do not want to attract the wrong applicants, and we all know the cost of getting this right or wrong. All this is about knowing what qualities and qualifications are necessary for your journey. It is simple to say, and less easy to do, but your belief and ambition should be detailed, known and, where appropriate, communicated throughout your organisation. Your identity should then perfectly shadow and emphasise these beliefs and ambitions if it is to contribute towards your aims, rather than get in the way.

INSTINCTS AND EMOTIONS

How can we learn to understand the instincts and emotions of our audience? Selfish as it sounds, you might like to think about listening to yourself first. By doing so we can reflect upon our own instincts and emotions in order to understand those of others. We may prefer our personal self-image as someone unmoved by emotional reactions to such things as the appearance of people, products, advertisements or environments – for example dress sense or the depth of pile carpet in a reception area. We may pride ourselves that we have the ability or experience to 'see through' and decide for ourselves the salient information and truth that we seek. However, the reality is that we are all, some more than others, susceptible to our emotions and desires. And it is in this morass of emotion versus reason that an identity must first operate and succeed, the most emotive component of which is often pure visual appearance. That is why your appearance is so critically important.

People tend to believe what they see. We all share a significant tendency to judge contents by the container. Moreover, we do this with a careless urgency. For example, when your audience meets you for the first time, or encounters your publicity material, they will attempt to evaluate you as speedily as they can, so they may proceed – with or without you. You had better assume that any audience is impatient and has a limited attention span. Their desire will be to label you, and identify and file this image with some urgency. Of course, likewise, you will be evaluating them. These snap judgements will follow a mixture of conscious and unconscious reason and emotion. And they will be quick: a few seconds or a few minutes. While the clock is running, each increment of time will make first impressions recede into history. In other words, unless you start from the correct position of identity, your failure will proceed, and compound, at the rate of one second per second. History will become track record, and track record, eventually, will become the reality of your relationship.

appearances usually carry more weight than what you actually say, but don't count on it

Any audience will also judge what you say against how you appear. So now it is no longer how you look, but also the content, style and delivery of what you say. It will also be compared to what you actually do. On these deceptively simple comparisons of show, tell and do they will be inclined to base their trust or distrust. As a frequent albeit general question, it is worth asking yourself whether your audience is likely to believe what you say when they compare it with what they can see. Consider that empires have been won and lost on the emotive impact of one picture or the turn of a just few words. A telling picture can dictate future events but, too easily dismissed by those who utter them, words can prove more telling than your actions. Realise, however, that audience reaction to what they see is likely to be the main influence over their first impressions. In other words, appearances usually carry more weight than what you actually say, but don't count on it.

What people see is both rapidly and for the most part automatically processed by their minds. They may not be exercising any concentrated or conscious reason whilst they gaze in your direction, but they are assessing you at the speed of light. They, you, cannot help this process. This is why reviewing your operational strategy through the eye of your identity, as though you yourself were one of your own audience, can allow you to explore and verify all your operations, and in a manner that is impossible to replicate from any other more traditional standpoint. Instincts and emotions are powerful forces, for they have a tendency to sweep away everything in their path – and that includes carefully manicured cashflow projections and obsolete organisational structures. To succeed in building a relationship with an audience, that is your key audience, your likely customers, you must either confirm or overthrow their instincts. Your audience's opinions are what will eventually confirm your business model's success. If these opinions are in part guided through your identity, so it is a significant part of your overall operation, that should be dealt with far more seriously than is commonly the case. The more exceptionally you perform in this area, the more easily your margins will grow and, furthermore, in contrast to the more physical limitations of manufacturing and distribution, this particular opportunity for growth can be attained more economically. In other words, creating and then managing a productive identity is cheap when compared to the potential costs of product design and distribution. Furthermore, for many businesses with limited potential for achieving true market differential,

effective identity is often the least expensive way to build differential and profit

an effective identity may be the fastest and least expensive way of gaining that differential or, for some, perhaps the only genuine way of gaining market awareness and sales.

Think of it this way: your audience wants to profit from your identity in terms of pleasure or information – they must appreciate a desirable difference or else they may destroy you. Just turning their back on you is a form of destruction, and that is assuming their negativity is not also broadcast by them to all and sundry within their peer group. An average identity is more than unhelpful here, unless you deliberately want to run the gauntlet. Furthermore this level of negotiation is greater than you may initially think; destiny is often decided from the first moment of eye contact. To demonstrate the power of visual instinct and emotion, spend a few moments completing Tests 1 and 2.

Test 1

Bank A

Bank B

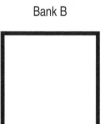

Bank C

Test 1

Imagine that the three shapes illustrated opposite are logos,
each representing a major banking organisation.

▍ In your opinion, which bank is currently increasing its market share?

▍ In your opinion, which bank is the most secure?

▍ In your opinion, which bank is the most old-fashioned?

Test 2

For this test, imagine the racing colours of four competing motor-racing teams.

▍ In your opinion, which motor-racing team has the best driver?

▍ In your opinion, which motor-racing team is last year's championship winner?

▍ In your opinion, which motor-racing team will fail to reach the finish line?

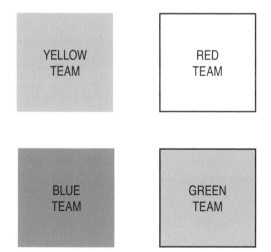

You may be surprised at your reactions to these simple tests. Notice that your initial responses will defy a wholly rational and, within the realms of rational, a defendable explanation. However, they may confirm or deny your personal preferences and prejudices regarding the appearance of both shape and colour. In other words, realise that the only correct answer to both tests is your tendency to make emotional judgements beyond any conscious reasoning. Your opinion has been influenced by the use of shape and colour.

Test 3

Here is a different kind of test. Imagine you a marketing director being asked to choose between four product names.

You need to decide a name for a new range of 18–36 male and female summer clothing. From the following shortlist which one are you inclined to choose?

▍ North Beach

▍ South Beach

▍ East Beach

▍ West Beach

Or course your preference depends on the emotive associations (the identity) of the words, product and target market. Again, notice that you are navigating your emotions. You may find yourself instinctively computing these word associations. Obviously, you reach a point where you will require a more complete specification of the products for market, and issues of geographic and demographic distribution. You also feel you need to do some market research: in other words, request the emotional responses of a sample audience. The upshot is that you are, of course, navigating via emotion.

Emotion and opinions (including those not necessarily rooted in reason) tend to lead the human race, and it is important to realise the extent of this before we progress to Chapter 2.

Jargon

This book is not a substitute for a dictionary or a history lesson, but some clarification of the word 'brand' will help, if only because the word is used so widely nowadays and often without enough thought, to the point where its lack of definition can impede the progress of the marketing operation. Using the word more selectively will help you to debunk a good deal of current marketingspeak, both published on bookshelves and discussed in team meetings. Leadership and management must always be wary of the jargon we accept into our decision-making processes, otherwise we might obscure clarity of thought and action.

critical understanding is crucial advantage

So where did this word come from? 'Brand' originally meant 'torch'. To fire an item fresh in the furnace was to brand. So a brand was a flaming torch and it became applicable to all things new. It was also customary to mark offending vagabonds with a red-hot iron either on the chest or left cheek. Until 1879 army deserters were also 'branded' below their left nipple with either a D for Deserter or BC for Bad Character. During this time a merchant's or excise mark on a commodity or article also became known as a brand. Then cowboys arrived on our cinema screens and branding became the burnt mark of ownership on cattle hides and stock. The good guy finding and shooting the rustlers somehow sticks in the cranium, and off the world goes talking about this brand or that brand or issues of branding, with no division between what identity means on the one hand and branding means on the other.

To most people this will be of no concern. However, to all those leading their organisations and products forward this confusion is worthy of some examination, because there is a division between an identity and a brand that is (at times) crucial to how you might budget for and implement your marketing strategy. The point is that, although in most respects a brand is just an identity – the two words sounding casually interchangeable – there is a significant inference in a brand, which travels far beyond just a 'plain' identity.

Like the difference between the words 'leadership' and 'management', 'identity' and 'brand' also have differences for those sharp enough to see the opening and closure such a difference can usher in. For example, effective leadership is deciding best direction, whereas effective management is deciding best actions in the service of that direction. In this respect leadership is the 'first creation' and management the second, and if they act in harmony the result is success. Confusing these two functions has obvious dangers. It might mean management overruling leadership, or a leadership unwilling to trust or delegate to those with better management skills than their own. Of course, the successful organisation is one where leadership and management seemingly act as one; the marriage is perfect and to those outside the organisation the two act as one. Those that understand these differences give themselves a crucial advantage.

to qualify as a brand, the product and its identity should be inseparable

PERFECT FUSION

Therefore you will benefit from thinking about your product in terms of it being your 'first creation', the identity you dress it in as your second and if you successfully fuse the product and its identity together, you will arrive at your ultimately most powerful creation: your own true brand. This brand is an enforcement of apparent reality – an extension beyond merely just a product and its identity, but only possible if both join together convincingly. If so, then you warrant the upgrade from those who pretend to those who no longer need to. Like good management, good branding focuses on the join: between product and identity, in the interests of making this so seamless that the audience cannot honestly tell the exact difference between one and the other.

For example they buy the supercar and the badge, but are uncertain in their confusion as to what holds the greatest value, supercar or badge, for each seems to inherently arrive at its value from the other. Product and identity at this level of perception are inseparable. For those marketers not willing to benefit from the differential between these two simple words, identity and brand, nor see the fundamental relevance of how product should merge absolutely into the identity and vice versa, striving for true brand status becomes an unproductive and accidental affair. Meanwhile deeper identity management knows the pathway to that which it is seeking to build.

To the marketplace itself none of these definitions necessarily makes any difference, except all audiences instinctively (albeit unconsciously) know that a true brand is a unity of product and identity joined beyond the point where one is merely tacked onto the other. It is a complete fusion of the two, to the point where the audience can no longer tell the difference between identity and product, promise and delivery. This joining in wedlock is so complete that no identifiable pretence, divide or surface wallpapering over the cracks can be seen. If the division between product and identity becomes apparent, the illusion is over, and the potential of creating and then leveraging a sense of brand is over. The brand that allows a parting to become apparent overnight becomes the falling star.

pretending brand status is as vain as it is insane

The majority of products find themselves in a marketplace crowded with near-identical products, where only scant identity appears to set one apart from another. Each product is 'branded'; that is it has been dressed with an identity that it hopes will offer some visible advantage, and to many a marketer it may appear that any depth of true individuality – that elusive fusion where a particular identity becomes synonymous with the product it dresses – is impossible. The result is a plethora of 'pretend brands' (nonindividual products with a thin layer of identity) that fall far short of the potential power of the market leader, assuming there is a genuine market leader. This does not mean these products are necessarily unpopular, or not gaining market share, for they may be achieving both at a price: driven by marketing spend and/or offering themselves as cost competitive. The point is that this is the over-populated and limited race that most products accept as their fate. However, it is always possible that an otherwise standard product in the marketplace can be transformed into a true brand, providing you know the difference between a true brand and a pretender and that also you are prepared to find a way of improving your product and identity integration, which will by default simultaneously diminish your competition's status.

To those of you with ambition, be encouraged that most product owners are not prepared or else feel unable to achieve this leap from the known into the unknown. Likewise you may, with this new understanding of what constitutes a true brand, now realise that you do indeed own one, and that this new-found certainty of distance between your product and all those who are copying you will allow you to act accordingly. That is, you turn away from or otherwise avoid the trap of becoming submerged and confused with those who chase you. Such progression is to nurture a continual self-awareness of your individuality and how this must then confidently translate into what you show, tell and do. Again, this new knowledge means you can privately redefine your apparent competition (usually a revolution of thought brought about by the consequences of better knowing who you are) and act with far greater accuracy and speed than before.

one way of redefining yourself is to redefine your competition

It is also vital to understand that it is the audience that ultimately confirms the brand status on a product and its identity, not the originator, producer or marketer. A true brand is 'owned' by its audience, and in extreme cases virtually nurtured by its audience more than those officially controlling its identity. It is, by audience vote, a promotion in rank for what was previously considered to be just another identity-differentiated product, however clever its presentation. Through synergy and acceptance this identity enacts more than the sum of its parts.

The danger or self-imposed limitation for you, the marketer, is the desire to pretend that your product is a brand. This temptation is a strong one, and 'so what?', you may say, everyone else uses the word liberally, so why can't we? The urge is an understandable one, for of course brand is the promise of status and therefore an extra or more sustainable profit margin. Where margins are tight, a brand should make the difference of survival. But those who are seen to pretend only serve to highlight vanity, and those who do not know the difference between pretence and reality will also remain unaware of the real obstacles and opportunities ahead of them. One point is that illusion of brand may only succeed for as long as your advertising budget (ultimately fuelled by your investors) can fund the illusion. True brand status does not rely solely on a publicity machine though it will naturally benefit from the correct application of media coverage. A true brand thrives in the imagination with minimal or, at an extreme stretch, no advertising at all. Obviously this not only impacts on your balance sheet, it signals massive changes in your marketing approach and spend. The stronger the icon, the more persistent the rallying point. That is why even a defunct brand name from history, a name no longer trading, can still exact emotional leverage. In this regard, true brand is both an aim and a credibility test. The market will demand a brand from the distributor in a manner different to merely filling shelves with knock-down products, and the distributor will demand it from the source in a manner that changes the more normal negotiation of buying and selling. When the pressure to sell to distributors eases, it is a tell-tale sign that you are on your way to true brand status. In a manner of speaking, your audience is buying more than you are selling. The trick then is knowing how to fan these flames without blowing out the fire!

All other products and identities, which are yet to win this lucrative status of brand, are purchased because of a less stable or substantiated proposition. They may pretend majesty and ceremony, but the difference of true brand is that it feeds off its own fuel reserves, whilst the pretender requires constant resupply and stoking. One is predominantly self-propelling and relatively frictionless, the other certainly isn't.

A brand assumes status and trust, and can become more powerful than the organisation that originated the product and its identity. The child can grow beyond the stature of its parent. Quickly an emerging brand can take centre stage and capture the show. A good marketer notices the protégé's progress. Mimics will always follow wishing to borrow or steal the limelight, so you must build your defences. This is protecting the intellectual property of your product, but it is also achieved by defending your identity. Patents will expire, but the value of the imagery created by the product's identity can live on. Even when it is lawful for others to copy an expired patent, it isn't lawful to copy a trademark, and other elements such as domain names can only be given away through error. It is therefore wise strategy to ensure that your identity is synonymous with your invention, in order to extend the period of profitability beyond other forms of market protection. Where a position of product innovation gives differential and therefore competitive advantage, this advantage will reduce (or even be overtaken) in time, whereas the differential contributed by your identity can continue indefinitely, providing you attend to it with periodic fine-tuning.

All these reasons are why the distinction between the words brand and identity should be kept in mind, and why the unaware use of jargon in this and other contexts in your marketing operations should be challenged and where possible reduced to a minimum. Jargon without sharp reason is a form of blunt thinking.

That's why in this book the word 'brand' is deliberately and selectively used. In all other instances the word 'identity' is assumed to mean a corporate or individual identity system that is being allied to a product that with wise planning might lead to brand status. Instead of being told to 'brand your product', you will instead be providing your product with an identity. Given some intelligent means of integrating the two, and with your audience's consent, maybe, just maybe, you will be fortunate enough to give birth to a true brand.

Likewise all terminology and formulae in this book are as minimal as is practical, on the basis that it is superior knowledge combined with speed of reasoning that is the most required tool for fast-moving executives. The approach being that it is more useful to hold an inner compass of insight – a set of guiding principles – than an inflexible and over-complex route map in the face of rapidly changing and challenging markets.

Integration

ONE THIRD IDENTITY

Your identity constitutes one third of your organisation's total effort towards the likely success or failure of your organisation's objectives. The other two are: your products and services and your marketing and distribution.

When you examine this definition it may seem to be fundamentally obvious. Yet it is too easily overlooked, and too valuable to ignore. Too many organisations, and especially their leaders, pay lip service to the role of identity. Even if they acknowledge or already benefit from the importance they give it, most fail to recognise the links between each third which combine to form the effective whole. They settle for far less: an uncoordinated, partly functioning, untuned and unstable situation.

a creative mind is an open mind, and one more likely to turn a problem into a solution

Like a triple-engine aircraft your organisation may be able to fly on two or perhaps one of its three engines, but far less efficiently, and with a correspondingly higher cost in engine strain, maintenance and vibration. However, if each power source is tuned and synchronised to perform together in harmony, the craft can be considered to be in trim, and maximum performance and safety assured. Result: a pilot in control, and the bonus of a safer journey for all concerned.

The full benefits of a complete identity can only be achieved when each of these three sources shares the same objectives. They should all be contributing to and complementing the same ideals. They should certainly not be in conflict, or for that matter indifferent to one another.

EXPLORING YOUR STRATEGY

The big burning question for you is will your currently proposed strategy work? Will the formulations of your current strategy meetings succeed, or are they flawed before the outset by invisible forces? This is where viewing your strategy via the vantage point of your identity, and how this identity integrates with your objectives, can offer you an interrogation of strategy unachievable otherwise. Unlike those who view their identity as merely a decorative add-on, you are going to learn how to harness the true potential power of this resource and ensure that your identity works smarter and harder. You will understand that it is vital to do this because if you delegate the creation and management of your identity to suppliers outside of your organisation, without the intention of fully integrating this with your commercial strategy, then you have in effect abdicated control over a large part of that strategy. This is inevitable on the basis that just your visual appearance alone in the eyes of your audience is the majority of the strategy they will perceive.

a strategy is a remarkable prediction – it is a pledge of responsibility

Notice that when investing in themselves or other companies, most organisations think first about commercial management, secondly about financial management and seldom about the way in which their target company frames its messages to multiple audiences.

This is despite the fact that most businesses fail due to issues of perception rather than product performance or their real ability to deliver. Therefore it should be no surprise that issues of identity, presentation and perception-building should be included in all strategy discussions from day one. The purpose of this chapter is to show how to structure your guiding thoughts on these issues and to explain the benefits of doing so.

A strategy is a remarkable prediction. It is a pledge of responsibility. It is a bridge of intent, usually against all who would conspire against you – vested interests within your organisation as well as the more obvious market competition without. In the act of predicting we push ourselves to forecast to the peak of our abilities. There is always a conflict: you need passion to drive forward, and cold objectivity to remain on course. To focus a winning strategy the passionate and dispassionate must eventually agree. And, it is normal for all this to be conducted at breakneck speed.

Within your strategy team, great and poor ideas will compete. The powerful and weak will need to contribute and listen carefully to each other. Instinctive misgivings are often difficult to articulate, and the pressure to collectively and speedily agree is dangerous. If, as a team member, you doubt the promise, you have a duty to raise your voice, however untidy your thoughts. The questions are never easy. Perhaps the current debate is too limiting? Perhaps the perspective could be better angled, or the view moved closer or more distant? Perhaps these discussions exclude, through ignorance or assumption, other significant areas of concern that you are presently glazing over too readily? If in doubt, remind yourself to list the critical components necessary for the plan to succeed, and hunt for issues surrounding these essentials, especially the potential pitfalls that you might currently be – in fact, almost certainly are – taking for granted. Squarely face unfamiliar problems and obtain specialist knowledge where required.

You need to place the relevance and importance of your identity directly into the mix. The trouble is, not everyone in your team may agree. Managements may not see the need for, or feel comfortable about, including the advice of those they cannot readily understand (or audit) into the centre of 'their' strategy process. This is a sticking point for those who see identity as only a clever trick of superficiality, yet simultaneously expect to gain the hearts and minds of the entire organisation and marketplace. What they fail to see is that they want the whole but only negotiate a part. They may want the rewards of a successful identity, but because they cannot understand the audit trail, they may allow it to sink into being viewed only as a subjective and erratic process of chance. You wouldn't build a suspension bridge with the same mentality. Yet like all acts of engineering, identity has nuts and bolts too! If you want greater design certainty, then it is only a matter of deciding that you will identify the critical linkages, however obscure they may at first appear to be, and then construct accordingly. You do not need to be a visual whiz kid to achieve this. You just need clear objectives and an open and unbiased mind.

your identity should be as well engineered as your product

A NECESSARY DIVERSION

At this point you need to consider how best to maximise the creativity of your organisation and its creative suppliers. Creative agencies are only too familiar with contracts that begin in just such a manner, where they are employed too little or late in the process to mobilise and contribute their full talents. Often the mistrust is a fear of runaway budget and lack of validation to match the allocation of resources. Marketing, and in particular the creative contributors to the marketing process, is a distrusted area of operation because image-building and perceptions are less accountable than other business operations, and the unknown of this divide produces a climate where those above the process may try to curtail expenditure whilst all those working within correspondingly argue for greater and greater resources (arguably, but virtually always, not clearly enough justified). So when push comes to shove, it is commonplace for a creative agency to be numbed into accepting that the identity process (in all its aspects of design, advertising, packaging and other communications) be sheared away from the more underlying business fundamentals. Too often those larger all-pervading issues of product and distribution are locked away beyond the – threatening for some – reach of their creativity. Unfocused or unstructured creativity is a threat to those who are unable to understand it, and whether this is the fault of those judging its validity or those proposing it is seldom a clear-cut issue. Through such uncertainties and insecurities of management the strategy may meanwhile edge ahead but with these limitations of disorder and uncoordinated understanding.

Be clear that the development of a product and its margins of invention, customer interface, application, pricing, profit and distribution are all legitimate issues of identity. For example, price and product quality shape a customer's perception of pleasure and pain, and also contribute to the definition of market category and position. Identity can be created and applied to deliberately strengthen or weaken market differentiation in *all* areas of operation, not just a limited few. Identity gives you impregnated directional control. It's like a steering wheel on your dashboard. You may have one already, but this is the full four-wheel drive rally version: not only connected to the right wheels, but all of them, and with the intention of rocketing you with more speed than anyone else.

For this purpose there are three 'key averages' that you should remain mindful of. For your strategy to succeed you need to navigate just three summations of 'product', 'identity' and 'distribution'.

In the midst of any strategy it is useful to exercise your mind about these three areas. They will tell you whether you are on the right path, as well as how far behind or ahead of the competition you are. They will also form the basis of your true differential: your competitive advantage as interpreted in this way. Through this differential you will also define your competitive values and, as a result, begin to realise more fully who you are and what you uniquely offer beyond any other market offering. If the strategy discussions you are involved in are at times confusing, or at least bewilderingly complicated in their viewpoints and conjecture, you need a quick and ready form of guidance to gauge this position and speedily find the gaps in the ongoing debate. Positives and negatives can quickly be noted, and the likelihood of success or failure rapidly estimated. To grasp the potential of this process you will need to think about what these three words represent in their widest interpretation.

THREE KEY AVERAGES

The first key average is your product. Product is your body. Whether you are sitting down or standing, according to current science, you need one! Without product you do not exist on the ground, but only in the mind. The anticipation of future product stuck in R&D may buy you time, but eventually you will need to be seen, touched and evidenced as being alive. Product, real product, is tangibility. Ultimately, in the imaginations of your audience it is only the tangible, or the belief of tangible, that they will purchase or accept as reality. If your product is a service, and therefore not physical in the sense of, say, a dumper truck or pair of boots, it is wise to make up for any lack of physical or causal tangibility through deliberately coded presentations. In other words, weight what you show and tell with all the 'weight' of certainty and substance that you can muster. That might include using unequivocal colours, typeface designs, more coherent explanations and content messages. A convincing physical presence – evidence of cause and effect – however virtual, controversial or contrived, is a prerequisite of survival. Without tangible product, or the convincing illusion, others may not believe you now, and certainly will falter at some later date. You need product, and (what is more) it helps your progress if it is above average in comparison to your likely competition.

The second key average is your identity. If product (key average 1) is your body, then identity (key average 2) represents your mind. I think therefore I am. And if others are listening, watching or receiving, by whatever means, you might (though it is not wise to bank on it!) develop a meaningful presence.

The third key average is your distribution. The bad news is that a great body and mind are seldom enough. You need to get around more, or at least socialise in the right circles. You need distribution. The greater your effective distribution, the greater your effective audience. This includes distribution of sales as well as publicity. Both create territory – physical or emotional – and therefore the potential for demand. Distribution is more critical to sales

above average in an average market wins

than the identity, product, or that seamless combination of the two: the true brand. A bad product with a poor identity may still triumph, providing distribution is secure and you are safe on margins, technology, the waves of fashion, and the threat of market disruption. However, if distribution is your sole advantage you are vulnerable to a predator who may be able to find a way of making this redundant overnight, or else somehow turn your greatest strength into your greatest weakness. Current success might be fuelling complacency. After all, if it's always worked, the false assumption might be that this will continue indefinitely. A technology advance that challenges the current status of either product or distribution routes will disrupt and endanger your trading position. You may be smart enough to survive one disruption, but hit two together and you are history. Think of distribution in all its manifestations as the king of the moment. You might have a great product and identity, but if market distribution and supply channels refuse to play ball, you are doomed. The only way round this problem is to locate other feasible distribution channels, even if this means free distribution and intentional spillage to wholesalers (or even, shock horror, fraudsters if this provides an entry into an otherwise unavailable market!) Viral or more officially administered, distribution of product and identity is never an issue that should be taken for granted.

WINNING AVERAGES

Why are these three components of product, identity and distribution referred to as 'averages'? Because of comparison with your competition. Let us be crystal clear: your strategy is going to bring you into competition with others. This would hardly need saying, except the critical point is that your progress will be determined by a war of averages. That includes all individuals and organisations. Everyone has the threat of competition, including all non-commercial operations (who must compete with the justification of their existence), and it is notions of average (real and imaginary) that will determine the outcome of your objectives.

The first truth of averages is that above average in an average market wins, whilst above average in an above-average market means money wins. It might be worth contemplating that sentence again. It means that if you are presented with two alternative products, identical in terms of basic offering, status of identity and benefits of distribution, the choice goes to the one with the lower price. For example, the choice of accepting two credit cards in a marketplace awash with undifferentiated offerings goes to the one with the lowest APR. The only other consumer advantages (above averages) that can defend a higher price are identity (notably status) or distribution (above-average advertising, the card is accepted more widely than any other, or above-average exclusivity that profits a sector of the audience's need for social standing).

Think about this: a contest between the above average in an above-average marketplace reduces all to the same average, and means that the spoils will go to those with the most money to burn, in other words those who can spend or lose more money and do so longer than anybody else. They can see the competition – you – off the face of the marketplace, should that be their wish.

In other words: before all other considerations of resource you require above average performance in *some or all* of the three key averages (product, identity and distribution), if you are to be able to gain entry into an existing market or market sector and, once there, survive.

Having a product, however exceptional, does not guarantee success. You may fail for other reasons of distribution, or identity, or both. Having a great identity may elevate an otherwise average product, but is it credible and have you the distribution guaranteed? Having distribution is a position of power as long as you can defend or remain attuned to fashion and technology changes that threaten to weaken your grip. In relationship to your current strategy, and the role your identity is playing, you now have a lot to think about. Yet the laws of this power play are simple to master, and ultimately always accurate.

The second truth of averages is that if others cannot profit from you, they will destroy you. Some people might think that sounds rather aggressive, but then so too, in that respect, is the natural order of the universe. Some might wish it wasn't so, but on entering the commercial world it is beneficial for your immediate team to realise this and thereafter continually remind themselves of it. It not only means that others may bully you, but under certain circumstances of profit or loss, they might just walk all over you.

If you are breaking away from the market's present expectations of product, identity and/or distribution then ensure your target audience not only agrees but also is prepared to travel with you. Will it profit them? For example, a new distribution medium needs to be profitable to your target audience, or they will destroy you if only through their absence. If you are not going to profit your intended customers with enough tangible advantage then urgently think again. Nothing else will get you past this point of market penetration for very long. Witness many an early dotcom.

Another factor to be aware of is when your identity is compromised or censored in the interests of obtaining the necessary level of distribution. This may be a market restricted by established brand channels. For example, a revolutionary home security device might get to market either through established electrical outlets, presided over by just a few brands, or else make a direct plea to end users via costly mass advertising. Depending on the size of your promotional resources you may need to offer greater levels of incentive to third parties than you may currently be imagining, in order to navigate the current market. If you do not have the budget to build distribution then you will need to feed off someone else who has it already. Obviously, this may mean further shavings off your profit margin. Less obviously it may mean a slice of your equity too. It depends on the partnerships likely to be necessary to rectify this one simple word: distribution.

Elsewhere, main distributors will not wish to upset their prior agreements with existing and therefore more immediately profitable rivals. Exclusive contracts will not be broken on mere promises of greater long-term profitability

– they have to be driven there through the fear or greed of a market whose demands and movements are threatening to disrupt their business. All these blockages and many more in the area of distribution tend to tax both ingenuity and budget. It is here that your identity needs to be attuned to the disruptive drivers that will 'soften up' the market ahead of you. Trojan horse or battering ram, your identity has a unique role to play in achieving your objectives, and in this respect it can afford no waste or superfluous confusions.

Then there are those strategy teams who believe that marketing their identity can solve all. In other words increase the distribution of the identity regardless of its lack of appropriate quality. However, distribution of awareness is no rival for physical distribution of product. Physical always eventually wins. Sustaining brand awareness relies on proof of product and distribution. Identity needs the reinforcement of a distributed product or service that profits its recipients. If without it, all is lost the moment the advertising budget breaks under the financial strain. However large the campaign spend, it will fail. Swashbuckling your audience into submission of awareness may please the ego of the unshrewd investor, and even convert into some early sales, but that is not the same as sustainable trading.

above average in an above-average market means money wins

Of all the three key averages, it is lack of distribution that can inflict the gravest damage. Together with an ill-defined and confusing product it is the most commonly unattended area of concern. It is too easy to make errors of assumption on which product and identity so crucially rely. Furthermore, the way you engineer your product and the method and manner with which you distribute it speaks volumes about the ethos of the identity. Product, identity and distribution all help to define each other. All contribute to your overall perceived value and reputation. Issues of product and distribution are areas where identity can and should exert a tangible influence. The right identity can transform mundane product or distribution and turn stone into gold.

The permutations are many: great product can be blocked by poor distribution and/or identity; great distribution can persist despite poor product and identity; great distribution can be rendered irrelevant by them also; and great identity can, for a period, persist despite poor product and distribution. These few examples, and many more, represent complex issues, yet their inner truth is a simple interplay of these three key averages.

Guide your strategy by these and the promise and integrity of any strategy can be rapidly judged. Identity plays a key role in the outcome, potentially equal to and certainly integral to both product and distribution. Evaluate on the basis that to be exceptional in more than one key average is necessary. Exceptional in any two is also likely to be necessary if you are to achieve your objectives safely. But, ultimately, it is being above average in all three that will conquer all before you.

This is why you must integrate your identity into the wider mix of your operations, and by doing so you can now begin to navigate your progress and explore your strategy decisions as never before.

Objectives

HOW TO MOVE AHEAD

Here's the bad news: before you can embark on your identity and its creation or improvement you should first concentrate on your objectives. This is not what many people want to hear, for they are impatient to see or be inspired by some visible evidence of who they are and where they are going – rather than the more trying process of first thinking about one's true objectives honestly and carefully. The temptation to rush can be overwhelming, maybe on the basis that any demonstrable action is more compelling than pausing to think or sitting down to discuss. Those tired of yet more meetings can be forgiven, except here the issues are so absolutely pivotal to everything else that follows, you simply do not have the choice to act in denial or rush ahead

perhaps you need to fund a period of apparent inactivity

with abandonment. This goal-setting need not be tiresome, but at the very least you will need to furnish your creatives with the general objectives of the organisation before they start to formulate their contribution.

Commercial objectives are relatively straightforward to establish, until one requires inspirational and emotive inputs. The more creative aspects of how best to achieve your objectives require time for reflection. Quality time. Topflight management know that to be immersed in an ongoing, pressing and busy work schedule blinds us to the wider and more unexpected opportunities that surely surround us. If only you had time to detach and consider more carefully, then perhaps just a minor shift in attitude, opinion or approach might produce spectacular revelations as how best to take the market by surprise and create a more profitable future.

Question one should be how significant a deviation from your present route or the route of the wider market category are you prepared to engage in? A more significant departure requires a thorough examination and rebuilding of all the values that surround your present situation. In particular, is a revolution of your current strategy appropriate or necessary for the perceived challenges ahead of you? Often it is the pretence of revolution that we are seeking, or 'revolution enough'. Maybe you require only the slightest of makeovers in order to tune up and extend the life of an existing identity? Or, just maybe you need (and can cope with) the shock of something completely different. So reflect on just how different you wish the future to be. What level of deviation (and possible disruption that goes with it) from your present path are you seeking, and are your team and audience also expected to tolerate?

In terms of creativity, identity offers you wider scope often than either product design or distribution, simply because issues of what you show, tell and do are so wide open to invention. Identity offers the potential for sheer surprise and an emotive power often unmatched, even by the product it promotes or works alongside. If this is the identity shock that you wish for, the greater the need to stop all current methodology. Wipe the briefing slate clean, and make certain that any outside agency you employ is not crippled by too prescriptive, or late, a brief. Have the confidence to engage them in the early forming of the strategy, and if you don't trust them enough for that, don't rest until you find a creative source that your circumstances demand. So, before you begin, you need to stop. Let the motors unwind and hear the silence of potential glide in.

INTO THE UNKNOWN

We all tend to be trapped by what it is we think we know. Whereas thinking the unknown is more a process of stopping thought and following our feelings. This stopping to reflect and sense involves abandoning the responsibilities of the moment. Commitments make demands with or without concern for you. Maybe you need a clear day, week or even month – and you will need to feel comfortable with funding that period of apparent inactivity. Maybe you need to make yourself the customer for a change, or give respect to yourself and the same standards of service you would offer your best client. Now is the time to invest in self; to find your destiny. If others see your withdrawal from 'normal' routine as negative, threatening or otherwise confusing, and it is not possible for whatever reason to explain or pacify, then so be it. Even the most assertive of us need to boost our assertiveness at times, and act in the face of fear: others' as well as our own. In a sense it is time for you to be a little selfish. Instead of reacting to the opinions of others, and others alone, it is time to grant yourself some space and mental latitude.

'Normal' routine, demands and reactionary behaviour are the enemies to this process. Habits are convenient, but should convenience drive your identity? Inconvenience offers you a detour or time to think differently. Habits abound because of the convenience they offer – the benefit of repeating and therefore not needing to question your actions as closely as you might otherwise. Habits need auditing. But they'll do anything to avoid it. They hide with tremendous skill. It is as though they have a brain of their own. Which is the root of the problem: they dissuade certain parts of yours from exercising enough.

habits are convenient but should habits drive your identity?

Start by asking how many of your actions and thoughts about the current organisation are mechanical by nature, rather than freely challenging? To be systemised is often good; a worthy aim of management, but systems can also mask emerging problems. Be concerned when a system appears more important than the mission. You know the scenario: as a customer we experience the blunders and absurdities of organisational systems all too frequently; much as you might adore systems, refuse to trust them more than the value they were originally created for. The sell-by date of the average system is sooner than most managers presume.

Also, challenge the existing revenue streams in terms of their relative contributions, similarities and sustainability. Try to categorise these in a way that allows you to think about them more carefully than before. Do they reflect the true value you offer, the true interest and passion of what you feel your organisation does when operating at its best? What part of the audience are you more allied to, which part of the audience are you more in conflict with? Are the tangible points of your deliverables the correct ones? Look at the payment points. You can only be paid for the tangibles you present – the currently understood products and invoices. What if you could move these payment points? What would the effect be of thinking the impossible? What if you reduced or even eradicated what you charge for in one area and increased or introduced a charging structure in another? Obviously all these thoughts will impact on your overall business model and cash flow, but by allowing yourself to see things in a new light you may find the source of your current obstacles and a good deal of renewed enthusiasm for sorting out issues thwarting both your passion and profit. It is often useful to think about what you instinctively most want to *do* for your customers, irrespective of what you presently invoice and receive payment for. What part of your existing service is closer to your heart and the hearts of your audience – regardless of how small a fraction of your current service offering it may be, and whether it is currently a tangible you are even charging for.

REALISING YOUR TRUE AIMS

As you do this you will uncover the objectives of your identity. As already stated, and important enough to repeat, you must invest enough time, even though the need for a new identity may seem an urgent affair and the added strain of allocating a proper period for the workmanship to be completed may frustrate you further. It can seem overwhelming, for all aspects of the task seem to queue up for attention at once. Above all it is about acknowledging that your identity must sincerely serve your aims. It must creatively add to the productivity of your otherwise commercial and financial strategy. The identity is not a flimsy add-on. It is every bit a part of the engineering and detailing of your overall objectives. It should be structurally sound, and anything less serving your needs is a waste of resources.

Aiming anywhere else can be dangerous. It is less likely that you will reach your commercial target. Even if you do, how can you know if the identity assisted this journey or prevented even greater success? It is absurd to start designing an identity in this way, yet this is exactly how many organisations proceed: sleepwalking across the firing range, distracted, impatient and unaware of the role their identity is playing in their chances of success.

A vague sense of general creative direction, the wish to emulate the success of another, the blind pursuit of fame and fortune are all basic ingredients of ambition, and ingredients that do not set any clear objectives. Asking a design team to race away with no other information than this is folly. Yet both organisations and their designers being unable to prepare, beyond the courting of style minus substance, is a common phenomenon. Not my design team, you may be thinking... surely not on their fees... But how personally do you explore, and share, your vision in relation to your commercial and financial objectives? How often do you engage in abstract discussion with the one creative who improves you? What structure and values do you apply when designing the components of your identity; and apart from the mechanical specifications (such as your logo and its colour), what summarises and controls the essence of what you show, tell and do?

Style without a deeper-rooted objective is zero substance. There are an awful lot of applauded identities that, like paper ships slipping out of port, once on open seas blow or sink who knows where. This method of rudderless navigation means wasting costly resources, and begs the question: just how big is your budget? An even better question might be: how did you decide on the size of your marketing budget, and what verification of its effectiveness are you prepared to accept? It is not uncommon to find that audiences miss the point of the exercise as soon as the press relations withdraw; but so may your workforce, for what confidence do you offer them? Your identity may be worse than useless, more negative than not trying at all. And when you end up eventually revamping it, you might need to add the cost of the refit to the original mistake. It may surprise some, providing they could account for the effectiveness of their marketing spend, to discover their actions are actually counter-productive. In other words, a tighter, but more accurately aimed, budget might improve sales – doing less, spending less, can on occasion actually increase your market effectiveness.

You might like the colour. In terms of your proposed new visual identity the typeface may seem pleasing enough. A4 brochures with bland photography seem workable enough. Oh, and we'd better have smiling faces, use puns as much as possible, and a snappy 'strapline'. Now we're cooking...

No you're not. Cooking a weak stew with no body or sustenance. A diet of such bland identities and their promotion litters the world around you. They leave the audience feeling non-committal, because that is what they are: directionless. All products are expected to have an identity of sorts, or else they are nameless commodities, but this is no excuse for simply slapping a name on a product and thinking you have achieved your mission.

If attempting a second design, without knowing the dynamics of the first, the difficulty of the process compounds. Repeatedly miss and then your willpower will vanish, and a successful outcome becomes more unlikely with each successive attempt. Likewise, a design team on their second or third pitch loses their own sense of vitality. Clients drunk on endless presentations increasingly lose sight of reality too, and, should the unexpected ideal solution appear during this late stage, its acceptance or recognition by jaded minds cannot be guaranteed. In desperation, or to save face (or budget), an inappropriate solution is likely to be adopted or the project abruptly terminated amidst confusion and denial. Either way, you have misconceived and wasted valuable resources. Such events happen more frequently than most investors are either made aware of or else will admit to.

You are searching for the one perfect identity. Quite simply, the solution that best serves your dream: your organisation's strategy. Even the most talented designers have only so many inspirational hours available to them when beginning a new project. This is the period when their inspiration rises to meet the challenge. Like you they only have so many hours in a day, so do you wish them to work steadily towards the best fitting solution, or just scatter their time half-heartedly on alternative ideas (all the while thinking each one must be different), in the hope that one idea may spark some 'emotion' in you and your team?

There are times when to work on the fifty-seven alternatives will be the most productive and sensible course of action, but only when the purpose and direction of doing so is clearly understood. Or else all is so much grapeshot – undiscriminating and heavy on resources.

Like true love, you'll know great identity when it hits you. Failure to feel this strongly means you are off the scent. You don't need to interview the world to find your true love. You have clues, shared values and recognisable traits. Concentrate and work with reason, and however insecure you may initially feel about employing a designer, or creative team, involve them in this exploration. Be each other's psychiatrist if you must.

It is best never to ask creatives to 'pitch' without brief or fee. Even with payment never expect them to accept your brief without challenge. If the creative doesn't question your assessment of the situation (with verbal discussion or at least a defiant silence), think twice about employing them! You need to foster what should become an important relationship. Look for experts, but only those with the empathy and ability to inspire you. It sounds naive to some, but you must like them, and they you. You have a long and eventful trip to make – a shared set of objectives that should continue to evolve over time. You might as well enjoy the company.

THE OPPORTUNITIES OF CHANGE

A new identity is an agent of change. Effective identity divides and rules. An important role of an identity is to polarise the audience and act as a selection process for the classification of customer, supplier and prospective employee. In other words, it acts as a magnet, both attracting and repelling, however gently, through design.

It also ushers in the possibility and moral authority to investigate and change internal political issues of departments, organisational structure, job titles and descriptions, production methodology.

The benefits are clear, for in the process of reviewing your cobwebs, a well-considered identity promotes efficiency and economy, both of action and expenditure. It enables improved communications, internally and externally, by offering a reason to examine and challenge the ineffectual, inefficient or obsolete. Yet when starting an identity programme the opposite may seem true: it may seem like expenditure with no immediate, tangible reward. Do it right and the opposite is always true: because it strikes to the core of your entire marketing operations it produces and accelerates profit and, with continual review, continues to keep pace with your changing products and distribution issues, your

like true love you'll know great identity when it hits you

organisation and marketplace. Some service department managers, such as those not yet acquainted with the front-end experience of higher management or sales, might miss the bigger picture, as well as the point that they are charged with the responsibility of investing their budgets – spending money to make money – rather than simply spending the resources they are given.

Other factors may also bar the productivity of a new identity. They include indifference or apathy within your team, age (too young to start, too old), market or geographical location (too close to see the opportunity, too far away to believe you can take advantage of it) and a shortage of self-knowledge and self-belief. Without forging some clear objectives you may unwittingly become a hostage to some or all of these issues, and fail to exploit the opportunities that are potentially yours as a result. That is why you need to proceed with caution before you can commence the actual design process.

Leadership

ABOVE THE PARAPET

Imagine you are an infant in a crowded classroom. You impulsively thrust your hand up into the air. If the teacher acknowledges this signal for attention, and invites your contribution, you must then continue past the initial plea for attention and communicate with confidence and clarity if you want to make the most of the opportunity. As well as ability, this takes nerve, both of which you may be fortunate enough to take for granted.

Courage plays a major part in the willingness to be identified and in one's effectiveness beyond the initial threshold of recognition. It means inviting reaction from all those who notice your signal. Personally, you may be able to brush these concerns away more readily than other members of your team, but the point remains that it takes courage to state your opinions and hold onto your values.

Your identity needs to be able to defend itself. Your fear of being challenged and the controversy you are prepared to engage in is largely within your control. You can avoid both by adopting a low profile. There may be good reason for modesty, but, whatever your preference, you appear to be able to choose accordingly – or can you? – for even the silent get labelled. And the silent really are the majority. Not all are prepared to believe in their values, opinions and ability to argue and defend themselves, even when it may be to their great advantage. Fear rules most people all too readily. Far easier for the timid or unconfident to dissolve their identity into the mass of the crowd, to follow a trend, any trend, and thoughtlessly imitate other individuals or organisations whose clothes they'd rather be seen to wear.

How willing you are to draw attention to yourself, by which method and in what preferred manner you wish to deal with the inevitable responses, are a direct reflection upon your ability and confidence. You might have this quality but does your team?

Perhaps you may prefer less intrusive methods of communication? Or perhaps being within a crowd lends you strength and comfort? Perhaps being a me-too offers you the level of profit you wish or are willing to settle for? Or perhaps you find the reverse is true? What is certain is that you engage in the level and type of confrontation you feel confident enough to be challenged by.

Being identified leads to confrontation simply because your identity will inevitably confront the identity, feelings and opinions of others. Your willingness to assert a bold and highly visible identity may be tempered by your fear of being challenged. And these challenges are not just external ones. Inside the organisation, the short-sighted, the ill-informed and fearful alike may challenge an existing, revised or brand new identity which they believe threatens their dependency, position or personal advantage.

How well you manage these challenges is determined by your trust in yourself. Self-trust could be explained as trusting the ground you stand upon. You may say you want an effective identity: if so, get ready for the occasional attack, for you will rarely stand unchallenged.

Seeking a new identity challenges you before anybody else. This form of self-destruction, for in part any form of renewing involves challenging or destroying the old, can be as depressing as it is liberating. Instead, think of it as positive disruption. You engage with the probability of change, and in this new-found and freefall freedom lurks infinite possibility. There are many right and wrong turnings – as well as a

difference threatens the insecure

definite sense of vacuum: everything that you discover and choose to abandon creates new space longing to be filled. It takes a suspension of belief to accept this space, however temporary (it usually is), for 'nothing' is acutely uncomfortable to those driven by habit first, thought second. It means stopping or stepping off – which promotes insecurity – the flip side of which is freedom. If you are serious about your mission, it is a heroic struggle against the pressures of current routine, attitudes and dogma. It is not surprising that creating and launching a new identity is, for many, a traumatic experience, a crisis compounded by the difficulty of establishing a new excellence amongst the ruins of the old. Get tough on yourself and your weaknesses, or fail. Gamble on your ability to make the right decisions. Apply rigour and set off to search for and study the justification for all that pretends to belong to your current identity.

With an unplanned identity, you may have only a scant idea of the reactions you provoke. Inconsistency in the signals you transmit may draw an equally inconsistent array of responses. Alternatively, with a planned identity, you should expect more certain reactions: because if you regulate the messages on offer to others, you should find, over time, the responses received in return will fall into patterns and, more crucially, patterns that you will have the opportunity to become well acquainted with. This information you accrue becomes a further confirmation of your certainty. This certainty clarifies the risks you can typically expect and, with these informed expectations, the defences you need to deploy – in economy of time, energy and material. The introduction of a planned identity rapidly enables easier progress. But, like learning a new musical instrument, it requires a period of commitment and discomfort, which as a novice, introducing yourself to your new self, you now have no choice but to pass through. However uncomfortable this is, you must commit yourself to the process of relearning.

you cannot escape identification

It is fear of being recognised as different, whatever the rhetoric to the contrary, that prevents many from achieving the identity to match what they state is their ambition. Gaining attention attracts interest from both those who wish to profit from you and those who may wish to destroy. Often the identities, and in particular the logos, within many sectors of activity appear to converge. The more competitive the subject area, the greater the tendency towards convergence: for example political parties and national flags, but also most retail product areas, such as food packaging and automotive design. They gravitate towards conformity through fear of appearing too different. The frightened and insecure seek refuge in numbers. Conformity is a comforting magnet. If questioned, and in their defence, these organisations may feel that they are promoting themselves in this manner in order to avoid alienating their target audiences. In other words, they are acknowledging convention, or the notion of convention, as their guiding master. But often an audience may not be as aware, or as concerned, about these conventions as the communicator of the identity believes. Indeed, it may be the organisation seeking comfort. There is always the chance that the audience is yearning to abandon the humdrum conformity before them, but only the very brave will give them the opportunity. Either that or the unexpected entrance of new technology or other innovation.

Those who defy the conventional boundaries take the risk of temporary or lasting ridicule, or abject failure. Those who succeed are recognised as redefining the market boundaries, often to massive acclaim – though always post-rationalised, for they took a risk that others either could not see, or could not take at the time. And so others follow.

When attempting to challenge boundaries, sincerity in effort and belief – in product development, design and service – is a useful, if not a necessary, ingredient. A nonentity or 'non-identity' is an identity of fake, mismatched or dubious values, which rarely remains undetected for long. You only have to look around most town centres to realise that the number of nonentities massively outnumbers the presence of the genuine article. You may now view this as an advantage for you to exploit: the fact that most identities fail to add anything positive to the organisations that display them, through just such insincerity of effort and belief. Unwittingly they are neutral or negative, or just downright confusing.

To be eligible for something better, you need to consider the risks. Those eligible for effective identity become conversant with measuring the nature of the risks they are prepared to engage themselves and their organisation in.

UNCOMFORTABLE IS GOOD

To reach the highest levels of competitive performance, you must not only approach these risks willingly, but also explore them thoroughly. The boundaries the risks appear to threaten may be negotiable: the perception of risk alters the apparent opportunities which lie before you. It is both necessary and worthwhile to examine your current perceptions and test them in order to validate their reality. Creating a new identity involves confronting and challenging your notion of the existing, and through learning of your true differential in respect to all others you are able to reposition what was previously considered immovable. Identity builds perceptions, and therefore these perceptions can be engineered in order to navigate emotional issues that otherwise, if left to product and distribution alone, might be non-negotiable. For example, not only does a strident identity stand out from the crowd, it can also alter traditional notions of market sector and signal quite different promises and expectations. To take just one simple example, your identity can suggest a larger market presence than actually exists or mask a near-monopoly that you might benefit from disguising. All decisions like these serve to increase or decrease your chances of success, however seemingly inconsequential they may first appear, and you should decide that to examine an existing identity or forge a new one is therefore a matter of very real cause and effect. Your first decision should be to confront these otherwise apparent subtleties. By this attitude you will benefit from better knowing the reasons for your successes and failures – and therefore learn to profitably proceed from both. If the opportunity arises, have you the courage to achieve something notable and, having achieved it, the eyes to see it and the ability to manage it?

a nonentity is an identity of dubious values

The truth that decides these outcomes is that many individuals and organisations do not deserve a successful identity, simply because of the current inability of their management to take such issues more seriously and sensitively. Sadly, some would not recognise good identity, which we can also call a productive identity, under almost any circumstances. If this applies to your competition then by all means recognise it and use it to your advantage. Designers often lament to one another that their best designs are under threat of being rejected. If they are refused, that must be partly their fault for lack of persuasion – or else they merely whinge. Certainly some do, but the truth must be that those who employ them do so because they do not possess the same level of visual awareness themselves, however astute they may otherwise be. That is a fact of life and should not be the reason for abdicating responsibility, as client or supplier. It is your responsibility to build a team for whom such blind spots do not exist. It is commonplace for those in business to recognise the successful identities of others, but have no understanding of how to achieve the same. In other words there is envy but little knowledge. It therefore follows that it is the fault of those who fail to trust themselves or those they employ – a double blow if they also pay their wages. Usually the culprit is failing to exercise the necessary courage to lead the team they choose to surround themselves with assertively enough.

True leadership liberates those who surround them, even if that means steering them beyond their own limitations and refusing to take what other people tell them is impossible at face value. In the same way, good clients release the talents of the designers and other creatives they employ. If fortunate, they both may have the mettle to explore and share the results of their experimentation together and, in doing so, form a partnership of equality and exceptional opportunity.

Ultimately we surround ourselves with the team we deserve. You may think you deserve more, or less, but how can you be sure? Who you surround yourself with broadcasts your personal level of confidence and ability. Assuming the choice is yours to make, what criteria have you chosen in the process of this selection: family and friendship, levels of professional skill, age, sex, quality of aggression, ego (yours or theirs), no criteria at all or considerations of budget?

you have surrounded yourself with the team you deserve

Perhaps the best people actually scare you; it's worth asking yourself the question. The idea is to prick your pride, push yourself around a little, get rough, tip your pockets out, have a good laugh at your own expense, mock yourself, detach yourself from the current situation as far as possible, and be determined that you will attempt to see more clearly – and what is more, learn when best to persist beyond the point where most others give in. It is time to check the view outside by attempting to look in, see yourself through the eyes of those whom you choose to surround yourself with. Confused? Don't worry, it is all part of the process of self-examination. The intention is not to lose yourself but to see yourself clearly so you can make up for the time you are now taking in examining your navel.

Failure or success is your opinion and not necessarily the evidence before you. Failure is worth daily examination. Truly creative people know this better than most: the possible wrong, the apparent mistake or the half-workable may represent the halfway house to the ridiculous, or sublime. Being criticised, rebuked, or worse, can be everyday experiences for those prepared to voice their ideas. They look risk directly in the eyes and work with it in the interests of producing the remarkable, the exceptional. Examining defeat does not mean choosing failure as a route, it means looking for the finer entrances or opportunities that nobody else has been prepared to search for or had the ability to spot.

The solution you seek is likely to be beyond the reflection you see in your mirror. The elusive solution that offers the substantial progress you or your organisation may be looking for is often beyond what you see immediately before you. If you are blinded by the reflection it is only because you haven't challenged that reflection enough, or tried moving the mirror. You ought to disbelieve more often and attempt to view events from other perspectives. Don't be afraid to make a fool of yourself. Excessive pride is the biggest single barrier to advancement. Fear of failure rides shotgun.

The experienced know they cannot go through life expecting and experiencing only success. We must deal with failure too, for in failure we also learn, and future success is often born from fully addressing past failures. Why do we expect all our thoughts to be positive, when negative must surely, by the law of nature, be an average fifty per cent of the equation? It is worth bearing in mind that often the most spectacular and creative solutions arise because an apparently negative situation prompts a positive one.

Acknowledging that this sliding scale between success and failure stands before you, whatever journey you and your intrepid team embark upon, would suggest that navigation of some sort is a sensible idea. With every objective there are choices of departure point and route. Preparation is advisable. A potentially treacherous route is rendered more secure by a map, however sketchy. Suitable clothing and mode of transport should be selected together with enough resources and time for the journey. If you are choosing to employ a driver, a navigator or an entire support crew of mechanics, choose them with care. With equal care, plan your journey. Though it may sound obvious, this standard of planning should match the standard of the objective. It is no good attempting a trip to Saturn on a bicycle when a rocket ship would seem more suitable. But after successfully building the propulsion unit or having found someone who can sell you one, have you the training to overcome all fears and to pilot this exotic but necessary projectile?

If not, decide against an unsuitable journey. Simply do not start. Stand still, rip the map up, retreat to base, pack up or plan another route instead. Perhaps the original destination is too ambitious to manage in one go. A three-year journey cannot fit into a day – so prepare accordingly. You cannot afford to be excessively hopeful or pessimistic. You are seeking your own new realism. Comfort or discomfort, judgement is everything.

The purpose of this chapter is to make you uncomfortably aware that sitting comfortably can be hazardous. Beware of feeling too comfortable. Feeling uncomfortable comes with the territory. The comfort of security tends to disable the capacity to react, weakening the will to make the correct changes. Comfort often makes risk appear far less tempting. Indeed, comfort may seriously hamper your ability to see and judge accurately at all. Some organisations appear to change for change's sake, perhaps because budget is not currently an issue, or they feel led by the pressure of fashion. Perhaps their middle management, with less to lose and more to prove, attempt changes that they are unable to eventually follow through with due to a lack of change or compliance higher up the management chain. That is fine providing they tackle higher management head-on and are not blind to the risks of doing just that. The benefits of worthwhile change may remain invisible to others; some may believe they do not exist at all. Either way, to find out, the only means of transportation is risk, unless another has already blazed the trail. The hopes and aspirations of the crew and passengers may not match – even though you may officially declare the same destination – but have you the faith to trust your instinct and act on what you believe is necessary, regardless of the opposition within yourself as well as others? If you do not already consider yourself to be an accomplished leader, you now have an urgent need to become one. And you thought this was all fun.

WHO IS LEADING?

It should by now be clear that the ability and authority of your leadership and the fate of your identity are closely interdependent. Leadership from the top is necessary for the strategy of an identity to fully succeed. Identity defines the authority of the organisation or product and all those who depend on its rewards. If the organisation's leadership does not understand the link between what it shows, tells and does, and how this impacts on the overall mission, then the organisation and its passengers are disadvantaged.

No true leader is afraid of the questions or insecure enough not to reflect upon the nature of their current identity gap and the issues that surround it. We all have a credibility gap, however small or unintentional (recall Chapter 1, all identity is, ultimately a lie), but it is the nature of the gap and your intentions towards its servicing that count.

An identity project needs firm guidance if it is to avoid hijack, unnecessary delay, partial or complete failure. This may sound a rather gloomy assessment, but the truth is that the introduction of a new identity often gives rise to much excitement and controversy. This excitement needs management if both supporters and challengers of the project are to be contained within the bounds of what you wish to achieve.

Discussing identity within the organisation releases energy. It should encourage managers and staff alike to express their thoughts and concerns. It can give vent to many previously unvoiced frustrations and much of this can take the form of criticism of the current management and the issue of the identity itself. Tolerate this as a small price to pay for people's involvement and enthusiasm. Not all their ideas will be sensible or logical, but listen carefully, for amongst these opinions are the roots of the current problem to be solved. You should accommodate this involvement without killing the project through committee. The only way to do this is through a 'steering group'.

locate and explore frustrations

Internal resistance is to be expected and this can take many forms, from sulking and inwardly seething to outwardly aggressive, covert or head-on. Even though it may be limited to only a minor element, and perhaps easily controlled or rectified, you should be prepared for the added strain of having not only to plan the road ahead but also monitor all rear-view mirrors.

This is because a new order of substance may also be the arbiter of a more fundamental change of physical structure and attitude. An alert entrepreneur knows instantly that revising or developing a new identity is a potential catalyst for management change within an organisation that extends well beyond the obvious visual manifestations of graphic design. Before stepping into the ring it is wise to realise that reshaping an identity can often reshape the power structure within an organisation in unexpected ways and at a surprising pace. If a newly planned identity poses all manner of shocking questions, the answers may return a similar fire. Your sudden passion for probing questions, should it be untypical behaviour, may indeed be an uncomfortable experience for some.

FROM BRIEF TO BELIEF

The threat of fundamental change is a key problem for all organisations, but especially for those which require a high level of transparency. For some a change of identity may need to be a democratic procedure, fully consulted and advised at all levels. Understandably, they may need to fully involve and invite the opinions of their entire audience. For example, the change of identity for an organisation offering membership, partnership or allegiance to a common cause – and this covers a wide spectrum beyond just charitable organisations or clubs – may quickly become an emotional cyclone. Financial investors or emotional investors in an organisation, perhaps a loyal membership, benefactor or strategic partner, should be fully consulted, or they may be alienated from the start. But the flipside of consulting too much is that you may achieve less because of the possible compromises forced upon you, and the extended time which may be required. Here, as always, the success of the process is governed by the ability of the management. You need to decide where best to draw the line of democracy.

For others less concerned about the consequences, a blitzkrieg may be the order of the day. And between these two extremes the politics of change can be managed in whichever manner increases the odds of excellence not being smothered by mediocrity.

Whatever the level of secrecy or openness the steering group must adhere to, it should intend to control the hub of the debate fully. This group should ideally comprise no more than a dozen people, hopefully half that number. Regardless of whether you are an individual or the leader of a large organisation, you should include yourself and (assuming you are not also the designer) the design consultant you select, followed by a selection of other key personnel.

Your management structure may determine the selection for you, though, in general, the fewer people involved the better. Do take great care with the politics of your selection for fear of alienating anybody of significant influence or opinion. There may be jealousy or suspicion from those you exclude, however astute your reasoning, and you should try to prevent any pointless bad feeling, which later on may frustrate the implementation of the final identity. Argument and differing opinions are valuable, so do not be afraid to include the dissenters, providing their intellect ensures mature discussion!

The design consultant must, of course, be an expert, but also someone comfortable and conversant at management level, lucid, articulate and not afraid to make enemies should reason demand it – a capable leader in other words. You as well as they may employ teams of other designers and creatives behind the scenes; that is not of direct concern, but rather their ability to demonstrate clarity of thought and design management. A major quantity of the much-needed inspiration falls within their job description. It might suit you if they assume responsibility for running the group, providing your ego is able to accommodate theirs. Indeed, it is often politically convenient to allow a designer this grace in order to remove any suggestion of bias within the group, in particular the accusation of any unfair influence over events from a particular faction within the wider management team. In doing so, you usefully transfer a good deal of the initial controversy and concerns onto the shoulders of someone already perceived as being comfortable with creative debate – and possibly, though not necessarily, an external and independent member of the traditional management group.

it is outputs, not inputs, that count

The purpose of this group is not endless meetings. You are busy enough as it is without having the time of your best management and yourself wasted by anything other than productive debate. Instead, the leader should convene the group only when critical to the process in hand. It is a forum for discussion and consensus designed to maintain the momentum required to successfully complete the project. The project can, and should, challenge the present structure and effectiveness of all marketing and communications within the organisation and, as discussed in earlier chapters, the wider issues of product and distribution.

Another aspect of those you include within the group is that they should officially or unofficially represent different interested factions within the organisation. Some outside the group may feel more comfortable airing their views, in confidence or otherwise, with one particular member in preference to another. However, a member's inclusion in the group is also a matter of their contribution in terms of insight and expertise. If they are likely to attend meetings in a mute and ineffectual manner, do not include them! Your objective is productive enquiry, a gathering and radiation of the key issues throughout the organisation – not to be a lone motivator accompanied by a passive audience.

Allow the leader to interview all the members of the steering group, together with a selected cross-section of people outside this group, which may include suppliers, distributors and customers. The limits of this research depend upon the ability of the design consultant employed. You may need to supplement this information with more extensive market research. The larger the organisation, the more reassuring this becomes. It is a hunt for patterns of knowledge, the traces of which will already exist, consciously or otherwise, amongst your team. An audience may confirm the same patterns of understanding, but within your existing team the evidence will surely also be there. It is therefore the instincts of the leader to recognise and then articulate this knowledge that will bring into the open your new consciousness.

Gathering the thoughts and opinions of others should include a series of one-to-one discussions, where the interviewer or sometimes the interviewing panel encourages discussion about the current, past and future of the identity in question.

Use a list of set points to be covered by the interviews but appear to be flexible and reasonably informal in your manner as well as in the order that you approach these subjects. Avoid being rigid in your questioning or further discussion arising from answers you receive. Engender a relaxing atmosphere where the interviewee, unaware of the finer points to be covered, feels confident enough to share their experience, opinion and ideas without any embarrassment or fear.

Should the conversation skip from one subject of interest to another, or fail to run in exact sequence, do not try to forcibly reorder it – instead allow the discussion to run its preferred course, remembering to return to all subjects to be covered before the interview is completed. You decide this conclusion. There is no set time limit. Some discussions may conceivably run into a number of hours, others only a few minutes. Remember that the survey is not a mindless brain dump but a selective process of enquiry. It is important that interviewees are made aware that they have the freedom, without recrimination or identification, to comment as they choose.

Their vocalisation, however humble they may view their role or rank in the process or organisation, should be treated as both valid and effectual. You are inviting them to make their contribution towards the future of the whole organisation.

your objective is productive enquiry

The list of discussion items should include the following:

▮ Background – an explanation of the history and events leading up to the current need for this new identity launch or phase.

▮ Objectives – the currently perceived objectives.

▮ Opportunities – the currently perceived opportunities for the organisation, individual or product.

▮ Plans – the current plans to take advantage of or create the opportunities listed above in order to achieve the desired objectives.

▮ Barriers – the currently perceived barriers to progress, such as resources, cultural issues, the current identity, market movement and drivers, technology, distribution issues and concerns, manufacturing, competition and so on. Allow time for proper reflection, for many of these barriers are of an illusory nature. Pinpointing their exact position highlights not only the problems to be solved but the attitudes and character of both the interviewer and interviewee in terms of the existing predicament.

▮ Compulsory restrictions – what are the requirements of the law, finance and time?

▌ Client values – what values of the organisation do its clients demand, and where are the pressures for possible change coming from?

▌ Your values – what values do you, the organisation or product offer in return? Concentrate not just on the obvious selling points but the often unspoken, unthought or intangible values. It is important to be persistent in your enquiries regarding this until you get some significant answers. Be aware that it is common for organisations not to hold any board-approved code of marketing values, or methods of measuring the structure and focus of those values.

▌ Differential – what unique differences do you, the organisation or product bring to the marketplace in terms of the three key averages of product, identity and distribution?

▌ Price – what is the significance of price to the products and perceived image of the organisation? How does this contribute to current market share, and notions of past, current and future market category and position?

▌ The current identity – discuss the negative and positive impact of any existing visual or written communications materials. This can include: actual products, case histories, publicity, building exterior and interiors, workshop facilities, uniform, vehicles or anything else viewed as a shared experience by employees, clients or the markets, local or remote, that you choose to or must operate within.

▌ The current identity – discuss issues of customer experience and interfaces and interactions, including all relevant procedures, ordering, returns, and other systems that impact on customer experience.

▌ The current identity – discuss issues of current verbal presentations to customers or other audiences, such as scripts, greetings and other customer-facing audio communications.

The results of this survey should not be a reiteration of the obvious, except where pertinent to the project before you. This is not primarily a survey of the physical or indisputable aspects of your past and present – though you ought to attempt, here or elsewhere, to summarise those concisely in order to focus them into a common reference point, or interpretation of history. Instead, this is an appraisal and subsequent mapping of all current attitude and opinion. You are searching for the organisation's intangibles.

As a general rule do not over-concern yourself with hard facts and figures. Use market research only where helpful in further highlighting the past and current state of corporate or audience mind.

This process of surveying stands every chance of tangling you in complexity, therefore your aim should be to remain semi-detached, though committed, and as far as possible an unfettered observer, looking only for the essence, deflecting all else in your path. You are searching for the cryptic or otherwise hidden, incomprehensible or abstruse issues. These threads are often finely spun and hidden within what is likely to present itself in the complex and possibly sophistical beliefs and frustrations of those interviewed. Until now no single person may have been in the position to fully see or grasp the opportunity before you.

A good brief is like a guided missile. The guidance system should include a pattern of enquiry which allows you to cover the obvious factual aspects of what you need to know, as well as allowing you the opportunity to experiment and explore the more elusive issues which have arisen during the investigation and discussion of the survey. The brief should be a succinct document leading those who must use it to the most fruitful areas of thought and solution. The brief should act as the catalyst for enlightenment, and avoid being either unnecessarily rigid or verbose. It should communicate the essence of the challenges and objectives before you and act as intelligent guide for all. In this way it should close more avenues than it leaves open. And in doing so must limit in order to hit the target.

a good brief is like a guided missile

MISSION BEFORE ADMISSION

As you have been warned already, be aware that some feel impatient to skip directly to the 'creative' work – to draw a picture or visual – but *a good brief is the most fundamentally creative element of all*. Later on, any persistent failure in the design stage can be rightly blamed on the weaknesses contained in the brief. Alternatively, you may not recognise the source of this confusion and, through the normal pressure to move forward, agree upon a less than satisfactory solution. Of course, less than satisfactory is less than the above average you are looking for.

Obviously, resistance from others may not necessarily be well founded. Many an audience initially reacts against positive change, for the simple reason that they may not know or yet care to know the strategic, design or technology reasons that underpin your new vision. The gamble is that you are right and time will prove you so. Yet amongst these differing reactions and opinions you will need the courage to remain passionately involved but, in a manner of speaking, emotional detached and sharp-minded. You require the courage to admit where things are wrong, or require improvement, as well as the courage to stand your ground on those values and issues that you are not only fully congruent with but have now decided are non-negotiable. You will be challenged – make no mistake about that. But it is how impeccably you deal with those challenges that will determine your progress from this moment onwards.

indifference is a certain sign of performance failure

You need to be fully aware that many an identity fails over the longer timeframe, and often sooner than people wish to realise. These failings may remain undetected for some time, perhaps not within the first twelve months of implementation. You may gradually become aware of an ill-considered identity, because it will be understood by you or others to be progressively ineffective. As a member of the steering group your tendency might be to deny such a possibility, but notice if you find yourself becoming increasingly uncomfortable or indifferent towards your identity. Such indifference is a certain sign of performance failure. You may even become mildly embarrassed or offended by your identity, irrespective of whether you know fully why. For example, a sales team is always aware of the identity that clothes the product they are selling. They know, in their hearts, whether they are consciously or subconsciously making excuses for this identity; whether this identity motivates or shames them. They know where, but not necessarily how, this identity is draining their confidence and therefore their sales performance. Like a sports team forced to wear a kit, the design of which they abhor, such issues translate directly to the scoreline. The unconfident team tends to lose, whilst it is belief – that elixir of supreme confidence – that overcomes all opposition. Confidence, wherever it is rooted, and for whatever combination of small but critical reasons, wins.

For obvious reasons a new identity gains a good deal of attention. It draws critics towards you. It is where the internal or external dissatisfaction becomes severe that you may come under sustained pressure to withdraw or continue to revamp. If so, raise these issues with your steering group and solicit other people's reactions and opinions until such issues are explained away or noted for future action.

In considering what is wrong, you will use every excuse other than the obvious: that the brief has not been good enough, and that the identity project has been flawed from day one. And the one you may therefore seek to replace it with will be likely to suffer the same fate, unless you regulate your impatience and do your groundwork. During which time how much opportunity, credibility and advancement have you lost? Like the early years of an investment plan that stalls before maturity, you have paid dearly without receiving much interest. You have wasted your time and money, and owning up to this realisation will hurt your ego as well as your pocket.

Meanwhile a good identity builds from the brief upwards and needs no further justification. It justifies itself and flourishes with ease. A weak idea in presentation tends to demand excessive explanation or preamble. If a design team elects to present to you in just such a way, remain wary, with good reason. The ideal identity presents plenty of obvious scope for creative growth, so as to cater for the organisation's evolution and the demands this will place on the new identity to not only keep up the pace, but lead from the front. A scopable identity is one of stamina and staying power that suggests creative ideas and interpretations. In other words, presents a living identity mechanism that can, in our imaginations, be extended and adapted further into the future to accurately serve your commercial objectives. So the moment your team begins to enthuse about how this identity idea can extend and be adapted, it is a most positive sign. If there seems to be more potential for the identity than you can initially implement or even list, then you are on the scent of a winner. If it excites you, because you can see the commercial boost it may offer you, then it is a certain sign that this identity in the making might fuse itself with your product – in other words it holds for you the potential for brand building if used wisely.

Finally and on a more practical, but just as essential, level the apparent structure of this identity must suit and be adaptable to the present and known and future expectations of company ownership and administrative division. These structural issues are too easily missed in the early design stages, unless your brief is clearly relevant and inclusive of your strategic aims. Such vital matters of structural form will be discussed in later chapters.

Differential

This chapter is going to allow you to explore the differential, your specific differences as you should now understand them as a result of studying your key averages. It is these differences, relative to the current market, that form the basis of your organisation's true values. These true values are a direct result of your above averages. They are the competitive values unique to you. Most other values are, in effect, merely standards pretending to be values. The only values that should concern your commercial strategy are those that offer you distinct competitive advantage. More common values that might only serve to benchmark the market in general are of little use to you in this regard. For example, saying you are a quality organisation carries little weight in a market that regards this, important as it may be, and proud as you rightfully are of this qualification, as merely the entrance ticket. Your values may include historical reputation where it remains pertinent to your future success, but all values including historical ones need to be translated into tangible actions: what your identity will deliberately now show, tell and do. The priority and manner with which you decide what best to show, tell and do will be discussed in the following chapters – and the more subliminal messages that underpin these competitive values, your firmwords, will also be explained. First you have to explore your differences, become conversant and comfortable with them, and begin to see

your true values are your differential

53

why this new self-knowledge will benefit not only your attitudes and approach to the market, but in particular the eventual construction of your identity and its communication.

FIRST KNOW YOURSELF

Leader or follower? Within your marketplace which one of these two are you? It is not that one is necessarily worse than the other. You just need to face up to who you are and, if it involves a change, to who you must become to achieve the commercial objectives. If you are content to follow, then also accept that this will be the top limit of any product and identity that you may be attempting to forge into a true brand. Until you change your mind, you will become who you are. If you do not wish to lead, then you may have profitable reasons for not doing so. The point is that by knowing you can approach the market and target your resources accordingly.

Some markets allow or expect more diversity than others. Ask yourself how much difference your intended audience expects from the market before you. Even in a traditionally set market or one in which others may assume there is to be no further technological advance, could these expectations change? In your opinion, are there signs that they are already changing, or that the audience is restless for a change, even if they no longer expect one? How much genuine difference is this market sector prepared to tolerate within the bounds of social or legal convention? How would this marketplace react if you introduced an improvement to any one of the three key averages (product, identity, distribution) within that sector? If (especially if) others currently assume this market is travelling towards faceless commodity, the application of enough above-average can bounce a diminishing marketplace back into life. Your above-averages will have the power to disrupt, and this disruption is to change or influence the market to your advantage if you are careful about what you are doing.

As previously discussed, it is up to you to recognise, develop, and then selectively disguise or promote your key averages relative to the present market. These represent your potential for differential – and therefore account for where you perform above average. Other factors will influence these three

Illustration 1

same   same   same

same   same   same

same   same   different

same   same   same

same   same   same

same   same   same

same   same   same

We are all drawn to difference. It finds our attention.

Illustration 2

different

different

different

different

different

different

different

different

different

Everybody can claim to be different. Those who actually are stand out clearly.

key averages, such as price: you can drive distribution up or down as well as change channels. Culture and fashion can all influence direction and change.

Ultimately though, unless you are above average in product offering, strength of identity, communication and tactics of distribution you will live or die on price alone. Even with lowest prices you will continually battle with the greater distribution averages of others. For example, the largest discount stores are not necessarily the cheapest source of product, but their identity and distribution can out-trade any below-average competition.

Remind yourself that your differential is arrived at via your key averages. It is these that create surprise, controversy and notoriety. They disrupt normal expectation. However, these differences must ultimately profit (serve) your audience. The more you do this, the greater the wave you ride. Just make sure you have the cash flow to balance product with sales.

establish above-averages or suffer a price war

Once you have decided where you are currently above average, you can drill down to your unique values. So, for example, an above-average product means values of user advantage; primarily values of productivity. An above-average identity indicates values of status and style, of which there are an infinite number of values to choose from, but in all truth a small list of values absolutely particular to you is what you are seeking to uniquely define. Finally, but certainly not least, where you are above average in distribution defines your values of availability and exposure. Whatever the truth of your distribution prowess, the game is to turn any disadvantage to advantage. In other words, extremes of either too much or too little can be interpreted as the poles of desire or rejection, depending on your selected market.

Some marketplaces thrive on even the slightest improvement. For example, some sectors of industry quickly accept virtually any difference, such as the entertainment industry, whilst other markets need greater reason of secure justification and evidence before they will react positively, such as the banking industry. Depending on your publicity medium (yet another element of distribution) your market response can last hours or years. Difference will always attract a minority of interest however extreme your offering, but more usually the bulk of the market's spending power follows at a distance. It is this distance that you must bridge.

Illustration 3

product	identity	distribution
above average	above average	above average
average	average	average
below average	below average	below average

Decide where your current competitive advantages and differentials reside under the three key averages of product, identity and distribution.

Under these general headings, and only where you are above average, begin to detail the specific values:

product	identity	distribution
above average	above average	above average
= values of consumer advantage	= values of status	= values of availablity and exposure

Estimate how much difference your chosen marketplace can digest. Then plan on introducing your bite-size differences with clarity and purpose, and in accordance with your available resources. If you fall behind on distribution, a late-arriving competitor strong on distribution might be able to steal your lunch, even with below-average product and identity.

Your first line of defence against would-be predators is an early-to-impact and above-average identity. Creating a strong identity is the one key average that you have the greatest control over. It is normally cheaper to fund than most new product or distribution advantages. A strong brand, even a youthful one with little early financial clout to back it up, can ride a surprising degree of market conflict. Your identity can be as valuable for your journey as any design patent or other commercial advantage. This is because its early promise of value (or its historical passport of status) is speculative and emotional and, providing it is hitting all the right buttons, can by itself threaten a market disruption to your advantage. This means it can be almost as tangible (and, don't fall off you chair, sometimes more tangible) than your design patent or any other form of legal or physical dominance. Fear of market disruption, especially emotive fear (when is fear anything else?), will attract action. Remember as always that others will seek to profit from you or else they will destroy you. If the competition is aiming for you, then their motive

others will seek to profit from you or destroy

can possibly be swung either way. At least they've noticed the threat and/or opportunity. It therefore follows that you'd better be ready. Which means knowing in advance what your aims are. It is that self-aware thing again: know what you want before they dictate or attempt to tell you otherwise.

Wherever your key averages are under threat (all of them always are) the role of finance becomes critical. That doesn't mean you need an excess of budget, but enough to protect your averages far enough ahead in order to be able to negotiate. Your commercial difference must appear to translate to market share faster than your operating budget appears to be running out. You need profit, or enough apparent potential to survive, in order to convince others (investors or detractors). The bottom line is, as they say, financial. Business, charity or government, it makes no difference. You must be underwritten or appear likely to follow through.

As your early differences turn to trading profit, and your repeat orders (the first truly bankable signal of success) look secure, extend and assert your above-averages as far as possible. For example, there will be occasions when it may be wise to employ only 'enough' innovation to achieve early levels of audience surprise and acceptance, before more confidently extending your market differential. It all depends on how radical you need to be to convert the existing market, and retain a clearly understood proposition. Too much innovation at once can, if you are not careful, be too confusing or shocking to certain audiences. The level of shock you deliver, if you are fortunate to have enough potential differential to ponder such shock, will be critical to you in establishing your early footings into the market. However, once your foothold is secure, you may more comfortably extend the differential, introducing increasing levels of innovation, to suit market appetite and your need to profit. This differential becomes your growing persona: your distance from the pack, your individual and strengthening identity. The identity increasingly represents your main trading asset, and don't believe an accountant who might tell you otherwise. In tandem with a large enough market and a scopable enough product, it is the intangible capable of becoming your longest serving defence against all others seeking to erode your advantages in product and distribution. When all other forms of protection have been reduced to average, your identity can – if you remain alert to its survival – guarantee your market share through its above-average associations and reputation. Your identity can provide your survival in a market sector where all else fails to achieve sufficient margin. What is more, your identity can literally outlive you.

your identity can provide your survival in a market sector where all else fails to achieve sufficient margin

The less than unique exist because of another: another who once created or is sustaining the market. They do not plan to lead the market; they wish to follow, especially where the template can be copied legally or the patents have expired. Of course, most organisations are in effect following where someone else left off. Even the product innovator follows in the footsteps of those who forged the original marketplace. Realise how it is rare indeed for someone to single-handedly sow the beginnings of an entirely new market category.

SHOW, TELL OR DO WITH CARE

We all know that certain brands occupy territory within our minds. Some are more memorable and vivid. Some we will willingly dislike, others will leave us otherwise unmoved to action, some we might not be able afford to even though we covet them, and the rest we just might purchase. Amongst this involuntary occupation of thought, brands and identities attract or repel, to the extent that we might wonder who is in charge of our senses: our own intentions or those of others? Such territory of the mind is of course called positioning.

Present-day marketing theories concern themselves with building this position through the manipulation of marketing activities alone, and without concern for the underlying commercial proposition manufactured from the three key averages. It is here that marketers begin to lose the understanding of their paymasters.

Seldom is marketing activity accountable enough. That is why it is so often the weakest link on most management boards. It cannot often fully justify its expenditure or actions. That does not mean that ranks of well-intended personnel and tomes of literature are not trying to prove otherwise. It means that, despite all complex theorists, the best leaders remain unconvinced. Generally convinced by its inclusion in their general strategy, but generally unconvinced with the tactical efficiency. When the marketing budget is set, marketing will always argue up, and top-tier management doubtfully up or down. They want clear and rapid pointers. It is academic, ornate, delaying and unproductive post-rational or hubris-led conjecture they recoil from. Clear and rapid guidance is what they seek. The test is how practical is the guidance? Is it nimble enough to bat critically tactical meetings or other testing junctions of jeopardy?

You are now concentrating on your three key averages. You have the beginnings of realising what your true differential is. However, what you must now choose and manage as what you might best show, tell and do needs to be determined. The following chapters will lead you to find your correct path. They will also give you means by which to account for your effectiveness. Then you can gather a sense of position within the marketplace. You will be productively marketing, and the most important positioning element of all will be what your customers think of you, not the other way around.

The point not to miss is that your market position is

- Your difference, which is the result of your three your key averages
- Your content and focus of identity through what you show, tell and do
- The perceptions of your audience.

But it is your audience who will have the final say. The finer the relative detail differences between you and the market alternatives, your competition, the greater the need for either marketing yourself with some notable ingenuity of presentation or, in its absence, a higher level of marketing spend. Remain aware that over-relying on differential through your presentation alone can introduce the risk of short-changing the expectations of your audience: substantial presentation allied to unsubstantial product differential will only work over a limited period, if at all.

The majority of all markets navigate by obvious differences alone, such as north, south, west and east. More accurate bearings, such as north northwest are the subdivisions and specialist niches. In the same manner, walking into a department store or studying any industry buyers' guide, you will confront the major categories of today. They will be clearly signposted. More specialist information demands greater audience participation: you need to enquire further. What you seek may not be in the directory. Not only might there not be an entry, there might not even be a present category. Are you big enough or bold enough to create a new one? Yes or no?

Think carefully, for this is how the majority of products fail themselves: It is 3pm in the afternoon. I've had a dreadful day so far. I am tired, irritable, and after this meeting I have a stack of other issues all causing me acute anxiety in one form or another. I have no idea when I shall be able to get home, and when I do so, whether I will be able to relax or not. I am not sure whether I am in the right job, whether my partner loves me, whether my children will pass their exams this year, or if I locked the door when I left home this morning. I've been thinking of changing the car, I still haven't booked a holiday, the boss wants to see me later and I am not sure why. It's also Christmas next week, and I haven't had time for any shopping. You are sitting opposite me ready to make your presentation. I have a note somewhere of your name, and I recall I must have agreed to this presentation some time ago. What have you got to say to me?

Something different I hope. Whatever it is, it needs to be ultra concise, relevant and interesting. It needs to offer a genuine and beneficial difference worth the effort I may be expected to invest. I not only need to understand you, I should want to. It is not my responsibility. It is yours.

Such is the litter of nonsense surrounding the market; it is no surprise that the majority of all audiences will scan your surface for the more obvious telltale signs of signal and need. No reading or confusion unworthy of investigation pushes you off the radar. You think you are in the market, but they don't take any notice. The alternative would be an audience who believed or fully engaged in everything everyone has to show or tell us, and that would include opening and fully reading all junk mail and studying all terms and conditions in minute detail. Gullible or thorough, the choice is yours. Even if you have been notified this morning of a winning ticket entitling you to millions in prize money you may have reason to doubt. Such is the modern consumer that even this may be overlooked or dismissed as a deceptive or empty marketing ploy. If you are the supplier of the junk mail you feel more inclined to examine all such detail more attentively, though it also has to be said that very few product managers – users of direct mail or not – ever view or read their promotions from their consumers' perspective. If they did, more leaflets and brochures would be readable and enjoyable; more websites would allow you to navigate more quickly and error free than they do and TV viewers would look forward to viewing this week's advertisements. The truth is that most identities shamelessly place their interpretation of their difference first, and simply fail to listen enough. A genuine and noticeable difference will open any door: difference gains our attention. It is then that a profitable distraction becomes your magnet: the show, tell and do of your three key averages.

All actions and interactions are the proof of position that consumers will experience and judge you by. This cannot be truer than when a potential customer encounters your physical presence. A representative dressed and voiced unsympathetically to the ethos of the identity will inhibit both you and customer. A bad telephone or Internet experience can do much more than reverse the intended position of any identity. Your hit rate might go up, when just maybe it ought to be going down. Likewise, if you are positioned as being caring and intelligent and your staff training fails to consistently achieve either, then you are unlikely to fool anybody except the less caring and more stupid than you. Your physical truth is your ultimate position. It is this truth that will ultimately win over all other persuasions of product, identity and distribution.

It comes as no surprise to find that the authentic act of caring will be remembered, and remembered fondly. We will willingly publicise the virtuous. Yet, how few organisations ever achieve this! To actually care, rather than merely say that you do, is one of the most inexpensive commodities, yet few manage such a simple act. A few kind words, a genuinely cheerful and unconditional concern can work wonders. It is rare enough to be remarkable, and remarkable is a priceless differentiation that benefits preference and patronage, and often a premium of margin undefendable by any other means.

NEGOTIATING A UNIQUE POSITION

Market categories and sub-categories multiply, and the central perceptions and contents of these markets is evolving and often colliding. So if you are sitting in the middle of the market, it's best not to get too complacent! There's no motionless. Nothing stands still. Yet at times we are likely to believe otherwise.

If the masses elect you, then they might thereafter expect you to follow their massed demands. An elected government has need to adhere to both the demands of their electorate's expectations and the day-to-day reality of contending with all manner of other newer realities. There is potential for conflict. Rulers need to daily decide whether to follow market demand or lead it elsewhere. Those that succeed in leading are the exceptional, and before they can receive a thank you, they might realise that the task of leading is never-ending. You might get thanks when you retire. Until then, no rest.

It is best to enter the market through an existing category first, and then negotiate your position thereafter. You must begin from a fixed point of current agreement. Such as an entry into a buyers' catalogue: a brand's starting category must conform to what the buyer already understands. Then your difference will position you into a previously unoccupied space, adjacent to or accountable to the original main grouping. Your lack of budget might necessitate the audience doing most of the reclassification for you, but you have some small directional thrusters on your rocket ship: namely anything that positively distinguishes and distances you from the nearest competition.

Show tell do

Most are persuaded by appearance first, content second. In such ways we judge more frequently than we may care to admit.

To knowingly judge by surface alone is to be shallow, yet this is the method we all succumb to for the majority of our decisions. Do not doubt this or be surprised. To quiz the apparent identity of a person, product or organisation beyond just a shallow set of assumptions takes effort. Real intent. If you see no reward for the effort being asked of you, then guess what? You make a snap decision. How else are you going to deal with the endless number of visual images that demand your attention each and every day? You only enquire further if you believe you will profit in some form.

ask yourself: do I need to show this, tell this or do this?

This is not a slight on your humanity or reasoning, for such behaviour is understandable and, in many situations, defendable. Our minds are overwhelmed with visual and verbal imagery, and in order to make any reasonable progress in our daily lives we feel compelled to decipher as much of this visual stimuli into information as we can act on. Do I need to know this? Will I profit from knowing this? Is it worth the effort? This need to decipher demands our attention and begs our opinion. Our security may depend on our reactions. This is a constant and urgent affair, operating at all levels of commercial and social decision-making. Even a seemingly mundane choice, such as do you stop at this particular gas station or drive on to the next, may challenge the greater need of not running out of fuel.

Emotional calculation can rival the need, in so far as your emotion tells you that the appearance of one petroleum company is preferable to another, and that you may profit from one more than another. All this, possibly regardless of price differences, even though reason would dictate that all fuel is much the same and whatever the imagery persuading you otherwise. The point is that it is through this clatter of emotional decision-making and responses that most of your audience spend their waking hours.

If 'seeing is believing', then it follows that so are hearing and receiving. We all know of successful organisations of positive reputation and track record who thrive despite what seems to us to be a poor presentation and appearance. We may marvel at their lack of visual awareness, feel uneasy about their choice of colour or logo, yet still hold them in high regard. Such organisations exist and persist within all markets. If you are a design agency intent on converting the world to slick logos and fashionable colour schemes, such companies are your targets, and you might resist comprehending why they would *not* require your services. If, on the other hand, you are the target you may feel equally uncomfortable that you have not yet found the budget for the 'necessary' makeover. You fly in the face of trendy business, and yet your profits continue. Everyone is confused. You are used to being told that your identity does not look 'right' and is below standard, and yet your business is confounding the experts. Meanwhile, the design agency will marvel that such a company can survive at all. Insecurity abounds, but the greater truth is that there is more to an identity than what we simply see. Some companies are better off showing less. In other words, the profile of their identity works more effectively through what they tell and do. What they show might be of a deservedly lower priority. It might even hardly count.

the last thing some organisations need is a new visual identity

There are three questions you or your team should ask yourselves. *Do we need to show this? Do we need to tell this? Do we need to do this?*

The quick sum of identity is perceived through a simple framework of 'show, tell and do' (STD). You show your appearance, you tell your story, and you perform the content and certitude of what you do. Effective identity manages these three simple channels of perception.

CRITICAL PRIORITIES (1, 2, 3)

A professional makeover – a highly polished visual identity – might be the last thing your business needs. For example, consider a local store renowned for stocking a comprehensive range of construction tools. Such a business may find their visual identity (what they show) is far less critical to their business than their specialist range of stock (what they do) and their customer advice (what they tell). It is possible that their 'tell' and 'do' (verbal and behavioural) identity eclipses the need for anything more than a basic (visual) identity system. Furthermore, without competition, a low or substandard level of customer service might not be as important as what they stock. Customers will still consider the transaction a profit, providing their fundamental needs are being addressed, and no better alternative is just around the corner.

Given all of the above, why should customers be over-concerned by the appearance of the 'shop window' or its visual identity? Other than asking whether this store 'looks' like a tool store (conforms to the genre), and whether they read the store sign sufficiently well to locate the front door and park the car? Such a business might change its logo and other aspects of its visual presentation as frequently as it feels the whim and, providing it does not ridicule its customers' self-image or elevate the self-importance of the brand beyond the peer group it is targeting, why should it matter? For this business, and many others, a below-average (even an amateur) visual identity may be entirely valid. A corporate identity proposal from the local advertising agency might not just be a waste of money, but a fatal error of marketing communications. Crossing the road for no clear reason only introduces risk. Their prime mistake may be the temptation to show too much instead of what they tell and do. For them, showing may be the least effective means of persuasion.

a below-average visual identity might be valid

In terms of your own identity, the persuasive language of one of the three – show, tell and do – will be the most critical to you. Proceed carefully here, for the rewards of locating and knowing the priority value of these signals will profit you. Once known, you will be able to control the cornerstone of the identity in question. You can then build, change or selectively destroy with both precision and economy. In other words, make it more productive.

To find the most significant of the three, find the one component or communication item that carries the main weight of your identity on its shoulders. It will be an item that stands between you and the potential for new business. It will be an item of strategic importance. It is either an item of presentation or, depending on your business, it may be the product itself. The existence and quality of this item will be absolutely critical to your business. You may have a product, but without this item your business is in danger. It might be anything from your poster site(s), to your brochure, catalogue or website. If you are a freight company it might even be your vehicles. It may be your customer service record, your knowledge base, the appearance and manner of your representatives, or your price. It might be a particular exhibition or series of events. It might just be the sound of your voice, the content of what you say, the words you write, or the innovations you perform. It may be just a few key business relationships. It may be your technological lead. It might be your stocklist. One of these will stand out above all others as being the single most important factor in your success, past, present and future. On this item alone you will stand or fall, regardless of all the other elements of your identity and personality.

on one item alone you will stand or fail

It is a good idea to list all such items that come to mind, and then place them in order of importance relative to the wellbeing of your organisation. Do not delay this! Do it now, and list at least the top three items, preferably more. Shown here as an example only, such a list might look like this:

1 **annual catalogue**
2 media advertisements
3 website
4 product packaging
5 stationery
6 office reception
7 exhibition stand

List these items in order of critical priority. What item is the most important for you? What is *the* most important? What is the one single communications item that you simply must 'get right'?

Every organisation has what can be called key marketing communication items. For example, to a holiday company the visual appearance of its holiday brochure may be the single most critical marketing item in terms of gathering its audience and closing sales. Elsewhere, perhaps a financial services company may find that the social behaviour and conduct of its sales advisors may be considered to be more important than its visual identity in terms of creating trust and its byproduct: profitable business.

Notice your communication priorities. Once listed in order of importance, begin to ask what general aspect of these items is the most critical. For example, if it is your website, is it the appearance (show), the information (tell), or the navigation to and actioning of product, ordering and delivery (do) that is the most vital aspect for your customers?

Of course, generalisations are dangerous and each organisation, identifiable brand and market has its own unique needs and strategy. The point is that what an identity 'says' – pictorially, orally, or in the written word – may be far more important than what the product or the identity actually does. Belief in a product versus its actual market performance do not necessarily go hand in hand. Perception can pretend reality. Visual appearances may temporarily be more important than eventual product utility or delivery.

what you don't say can be more telling than what you do

Your show, tell and do form the critical parts of the whole experience. Of these three, any individual component may be more weighted or silent than another; each has its own priorities to be taken account of. These priorities should tally with the perceptions we wish to arouse or enforce within the audience. It is these perceptions that help create asset value, through the profit that positive perceptions tend to attract. It is these same perceptions that precede market penetration and longer-term market share.

Behavioural issues also play their role. For example, are your staff demonstrating politeness as well as providing a competent level of knowledge? Are these necessary to achieve target sales, or do they inhibit your audience? There are situations where excessive politeness might, to your great surprise, erode the chances of a product or service succeeding. When it comes to expertise, it is sometimes the customer who wishes to be regarded as the expert, deservedly or otherwise. Customer domination or servitude can be guided by an awareness of what you tell or do. Tune it up or tune it down. We have all been on the receiving end of excessive corporate politeness, and all of us have at some time or another recoiled from what we have perceived to be false sincerity. Put it another way: balance in everything *is* everything. In understanding the basics of show, tell and do you now have the necessary tone controls. The emphasis is yours. You may decide you are a do, tell and show company, or a tell, show, do. The important thing is simply to know what you need to obtain the results you require.

To return to the crucial point: it is a fact that certain communication items are 'mission critical'. Without them working fully to advantage, sales performance will correspondingly suffer. One will follow the other. Meanwhile all manner of other marketing initiatives and procedures will be less pivotal to your objectives. Of course, all marketing communications are ultimately important, but the obvious and often overlooked reality is that a select few are much more important than others. You need to identify them and then lend appropriate emphasis. They will not be equal in status or priority of presentation. The correct emphasis between what is best for you to show, tell and do will never be of even weight or distribution. The best sequence for you is just that: a sequence. You may, on reflection, decide you are a 'tell, do, show', or a 'do, show, tell'. The potency of the right sequence for you, the one that will persuade your elected target market greater than any other, should be fully understood and harnessed.

So how do you achieve this knowledge? You begin by dividing your marketing operations into three levels of 'critical'. You can call these levels what you wish, but for convenience let us refer to them as Critical 1, 2 and 3.

For this exercise Critical 1 is the highest level of critical importance, and Critical 3 the least important. Generally, though not exclusively, these levels will also correspond to the general categories of show, tell and do. This means that, depending on your marketing operation and intended audience, these three elements will form a reasonably clear line of priority. One of them will stand out as being more critical to your aims than the other two, and so forth. Here you need to reflect carefully on your intended market and the likely preconceived perceptions and reactive nature of the individuals you are likely to encounter.

Illustration 4

show tell do	do tell show
show do tell	tell show do
do show tell	tell do show

By examining the nature of your Critical 1 priorities begin to understand your priority of show, tell and do.

The reward is greater certainty, performance and productivity from your available resources.

JUNCTIONS OF JEOPARDY

All items in Critical 1 must simply be 'right'. If they are 'wrong' or less than ideal, your entire operational progress will suffer, and your resources will be spent inefficiently.

For all items considered Critical 2 it is, of course, beneficial if they are also totally effective, but there is an approximation of excellence that might be tolerated here. They represent a lesser risk and impediment to you than those in Critical 1, but a greater risk than Critical 3.

Critical 3 is the most tolerant area of all. Items that fall into this level are typically those issues you would ideally like to deal with comprehensively, but it is not essential if they are completed today, next week or, possibly, ever! Some

Illustration 5

critical 1 100% mission critical

critical 2 tolerable approximation of excellence permitted

critical 3 non-critical; dimishing returns of investment;
            beneficial but not essential to success

Prioritise and concentrate your resources accordingly.

*an obvious
priority of action
is required*

of them may even contradict the higher critical levels and still 'get away with it'. Obviously it is best for all the iron filings of your marketing plan to be pointing in the same general direction, but when time and resources are in short supply (when aren't they?) one can pay less attention to these lower levels, as it can be broadly assumed they represent fewer associated risks or rewards.

What becomes clear is that an obvious priority of action is required. Some marketing items need perfecting with a greater urgency than others. That you may not be able to sufficiently manage all these priorities at once should be a truth acknowledged. This should not form an excuse, or statement of the obvious, but instead be an accepted reality. Instead of your paid staff wasting nervous energy on a list of desired actions beyond necessity or current ability, they can instead concentrate on vital strategic issues.

EFFECTIVENESS

Larger organisations may wish to measure the effectiveness of their identity. It is possible to score Critical levels 1, 2 and 3 and marketing components within these three levels – this will be more fully discussed in Chapter 9, *Firmwords*.

This creates an audit of what the imagery, messages and actions project to an audience. In other words, instead of just measuring end sales, response rates or other end-of-process receipts, you can measure the communications as they leave the stable. If you are a smaller organisation you may prefer to use your self-knowledge of show, tell and do and their critical levels as a ready reckoner, a simple guidance system to reassure you. Either way, your marketing priorities of expenditure, and their levels of need and effectiveness, can now be rationalised against a structure of intent and, furthermore, one that can be understood as a sound basis of logic in any boardroom.

The proposed 'truth' of your identity demands management. This is the divide between the mask you present to your audience, and the actual experience of product or service you offer. It is the gap of profit or loss that we discussed in Chapter 1.

For some organisations and products the quality of the experience they offer exceeds the promise of their appearance. In other words they are noticeably better than their identity indicates. Here the harm is a self-inflicted lost opportunity. Those clients that knowingly accept the shortcomings of such an organisation's identity may be bemused or enthused by their 'discovery'. They may spread the word or keep the secret – possibly through the fear that rising demand might destroy the source, or because they consider the organisation is unable to sustain the subsequent growth, or perhaps the potential of mass popularity offends their elitist taste. For other organisations these roles can be reversed: their identity promises more than their product or service delivers. This can be forgiven, providing it is also credible – the gap between the promise and the reality is understandable or bearable because the promise remains sincere. Of course, patience can only be stretched so far. If waiting or enduring too long, those disappointed finally flee, and persuading them to return may be a lengthy and difficult exercise.

manage your truth or truth will surely manage you

The integrity or corruption of your identity, in the eyes and ears of the audience, is determined by how well you manage this duality. The danger arises when the credibility break appears or becomes unsustainable. A tired or cynical audience may reach a point where the divide becomes too large for comfort. This is the beginning of a major identity crisis. To recover, you must understand the problem and react quickly for disbelief can become permanent, and the identity together with your reputation consigned to history.

IDENTITY DRIVERS

So to what purpose do you address what you ought best to show, tell and do? What are the drivers, the 'buttons' of action, the likely pressures and needs of your audience, and how best do you harness those drivers in order to maximize their response?

For some this may seem a little negative, but it will help you in simple terms to realise that it is security that drives all markets. Even the need to survive is driven by the insecurity of what happens if you can't. Needs, investments, wants, desires, obsessions, decisions, relationships, politics, law, health, education, defence, productivity, rising and falling prices – and anything else you care to ponder deeply enough – are all rooted in issues of security. Of course that is a big sweeping statement, but explore the benefits of understanding market drivers in this simple a way.

Understand the confusion of the market before you and the emotional reactions that most audiences succumb to. First, notice that the majority of identities do not declare any clear promise or proposition. Most confuse product offering and category. It often seems more trouble than it is worth to either understand the offering or the service they provide. Furthermore, studying their literature or being unfortunate enough to encounter an insufficiently trained sales assistant might only serve to confuse you further. Most presentation is less than helpful.

the first base of your identity must concern security

It's as though you are expected to know the answers already, and you may feel insecure enough to imagine that the ignorance is yours – your fault, not theirs. Buying, and trying to quickly understand, the latest hi-tech gadget usually proves this theory. How often has a sales 'assistant' impatiently or otherwise insensitively baffled you with jargon and inappropriate information? Secondly, notice how few 'shop fronts' fail to adequately explain such simple lowly facts as their true product and market category. You are too often expected to know already, or else left to guess! Perhaps they refuse to be directly associated with the nearest conventional market category. Perhaps it offends their feelings of status, individuality or ethics. The trouble is that such posturing or inattention can only restrict their business. Unless you are after a cult following, it doesn't help.

An audience's interest primarily stems from their insecurities, both conscious and unconscious. Consider that their conscious demand for security may not tally with their unconscious and more emotionally-based insecurities. The two can differ. However, for simple and clear navigation appropriate to our needs, these can be condensed into just three main drivers of love, fear or greed. Three words that are capable of describing a myriad of inner compulsions and lead to all emotional responses. Review your collective audience under the categories of these three drivers. Then concentrate the main emotional focus of your identity and its communication accordingly.

Consider a few examples. Love may be the driver of someone wishing to provide security for a loved one, such as an investment plan or wedding ring. Fear is more common, such as fear of technology obsolescence, sudden market changes, failure to be insured, being seen as unfashionable, unconfident, and so on. Fear alone may prevent someone walking onto your exhibition stand. Greed may propel them. Greed too is ultimately an act of insecurity, an act driven by the desire or need to allay insecurity and meet the apparent needs for survival, even if these needs are grossly exaggerated or misinterpreted. For many, market domination is the act of securing what they see as a limited resource in order to prevent others from eating 'their' lunch. Never mind that they can't possibly eat all the food. It follows that what you show, tell and do should cater for these appetites.

PURPOSEFUL DISRUPTION

You might wish to approach a market (consumers or suppliers) via fear of disruption in any one or more of the three key averages of product, identity and/or distribution. Detail the prime constituents of the insecurities this may produce. Be aware that one person's insecurity is another's opportunity for greater security. Disruption provides a potential point of change, an entrance

disruption is the entrance and exit of all markets

into an otherwise stale market, or the unexpected exit. So be most careful when deciding what you actually show, tell or do. Beware that the insecurities you introduce or address by your existence in the market, however indirectly implied, might be better left unsaid. It may be best to infer what is politic, not to say through what you show. Or it may be best not to show or tell, but simply do. These subtle variables become your route to profitable market share or exit.

If you make other market players insecure they might wish to sink you, partner you or buy you out. Through insecurity you become a significant threat, and so in this respect any reaction is a positive reaction in that you are by your existence making a difference to the existing power balance. Yet remain vigilant – fearful even – that if they decide they cannot profit from you then they will seek to destroy you. Even the disillusioned employee is a potential destroyer. At all levels and in all business relationships it is against this single knife-edge that you should hone your presentation.

Illustration 6

show **tell** do **love** fear greed

A useful way of concentrating your messages can be derived from knowing your preferred STD and then, depending on the opportunities and limitations of the communication channel you are using, your values and your morals, concentrating your content on the most appropriate driver of love, fear or greed.

Intangibles

By all means tell, boast or say nothing – but speak with care. How else can someone get to know about what you do and how well you do it? The answer is that they can know through the personal experience of meeting you or from what others say about you.

Alternatively they could ask you in person just how excellent you consider yourself to be, giving you the opportunity to answer as immodestly as you wish. Or you could tell them anyway, whether they have requested your opinion or not, by giving them a monologue on exactly how fantastic you believe you are. Maybe you are too cautious to do either, which is wise, for there can be a fine line between telling and boasting. Worse, constantly telling others about yourself, regardless of their interest, quickly relegates you to the level of a self-centred bore.

excellence is never boring

In this instance boring has little to do with repetition or consistency, which, in many situations connected to identity, is a positive force towards recognition and success. In contrast, boring somebody could be described as over-communicating that which needs no such emphasis. The solution is to understand the priority of the messages which need to be communicated and the best channels or methods for communicating them.

This is why excellence is never boring. Even for a dull personality there is a huge difference between appearing steady and uneventful, and boring an audience away. The former may be just what the audience wants, so they retain their interest, but a bored audience is one switched off by your message, dull or enlivening. You have lost them, assuming you found them in the first place.

For those destined or hell-bent on becoming an intriguing enigma, avoiding, censoring or being highly selective in exposing yourself from behind the mask of your planned identity – especially after achieving recognition through controversy or notoriety – can transform you into a powerful but elusive figment in other people's imaginations. This is a form of cult status. You restrict severely what you say, but allow your planned identity – what you show and what you do – to say it all on your behalf. Refuse interviews, give one-word answers, act as unpredictably and without explanation as you wish, yet all the while the identity 'show and do' that you elsewhere planned promotes you unashamedly, regardless of your apparent contradictions, usually because of them.

A planned identity increases your strength and opportunity to reach out to your audience(s) and can say more than you can ever say about yourself personally. The persona of your identity can say it for you. It is an opportunity to speak without speaking, boast without boasting. It communicates whether you are awake or asleep, there in person, speaking through a representative or have your lips selectively sealed. It endorses you, even though it is you endorsing yourself, for it works as though a third party. A loyal and tireless worker, it is a servant who quietly and relentlessly does what you ask of it and, subject to the abilities and limitations you specify when designing it, the servant you deserve. So before you start to construct your identity, make sure you deserve what you seek. To achieve this requires a rigorous level of self-understanding. The potential reward is that your return, all being well, will far outweigh your original investment.

Remind yourself that your identity contributes to one-third of your overall success or failure. Also remind yourself that it is one of your three key averages. The full benefits of a complete identity can only be achieved when each of these three key averages – product, identity and distribution – share the same objectives. They should all be contributing to and complementing the same ideals, and where possible promoting you as above average in your marketplace. They should certainly not be in conflict, indifferent to one another, or working against your aims. In other words, don't let your identity shoot you in the foot. The values that your identity promotes should

Illustration 7

'Organisation A are the best'

by Independent Review

'Though I say it myself, I am the greatest'

Organisation A
Excellence guaranteed

There are many of ways of communicating the same message, yet in a subtly different manner.

Create and choose the technique to suit your organisation or product.

appropriately support your strategic objectives. These should be deliberate and wholly positive. You have no room for negative identity, and neutral values promoted by your identity only serve to confuse and needlessly engage your audience. Your identity should be ruthlessly efficient, which means economic and advantageously powerful. Anything less is not only a waste of resources, but unnecessary risk and a dangerous complacency.

So how should the values that underpin your identity meet and support your objectives? To understand this you need to delve deeper. It requires clarity of thought, and possibly a little hard work on your behalf. Think of it in this way. Objectives are usually factual by nature and often definable by data, for example sales targets, market share or physical size. Values – moral or competitive – are more difficult to communicate, or their credibility is easily destroyed if you believe or say one thing and a fellow director or employee believes and says another. Unless you can agree their definition, launching an identity with confidence and then maintaining it afterwards becomes a less than ideal process. Therefore, any discussion relating to values takes an above-average enquiring mind. See the profit in chasing their definition and, as a leader, be prepared to follow this through. To those you seek to lead, definitions of mind are likely to be far harder to agree on than definitions of body. Yet you need to know the mind of your identity; the intangibles that underpin the values of your identity and which you intend to radiate to your audience.

MINDFUL VALUATIONS

Accountants talk fashionably of 'tangible' and 'intangible'. They are increasingly of the opinion that the intangible may often be more valuable than the tangible, which is a problem for the unimaginative, for it means accounting for the unseen: goodwill, brand, invention, patent and much more. Not that it should be a surprise to you: your mind is mostly intangible, your body mostly tangible. You can map your physical body a good deal more easily than you can map your mind.

So for tangible we can substitute the word 'body', and for intangible the word 'mind'. This is a useful word swop when considering the emotive appeal of your identity.

The characteristics of the tangible are commonly agreed upon. They can be measured in units that others can also understand. But intangible is a matter of the invisible: the uncanny vision, sense or inspiration, and a lot more. These elements attempt to defy measurement or common agreement even amongst those responsible for their creation. For example, the entrepreneur creates success yet often has difficulty in explaining what exactly happened. The book-keeper asked to evaluate and rationalise this success must realise that they cannot fully explain either, except by the common units and protocols of their profession. Here the only tangibles are those which clearly fit within these narrow definitions. Those who suspect a more expansive reality are left outside this consensus of measurement. Therefore the intangible remains an argument of conflicting estimation, its true value probably never officially agreed. It may often fail to even be acknowledged by some. It all too readily escapes scrutiny.

It is easy to criticise, for the taking of measurements is not as easy as it may sound. Some things lend themselves to measurement more than others. For example, you can measure history, as it appears to exist in accountancy terms by quantity, date and fiscal depreciation. You can also measure physical body or land mass – we can all agree on the measurement of a measuring rule, whatever the system of units employed. Likewise we can produce an audit trail of name, products in stock, location and expanse of premises, transportation facilities, plant lists, the estimated size of the markets you target, the audited needs of the audiences via the statistics of market research, the market penetration in relation to the former, the overhead and profit of what you have achieved up until yesterday, and any other statistical information you stand a chance of gathering. This data is important and has value, but that does not mean that it should be accepted unchallenged, for data is an interpretation of apparent facts, and there will be faults due to the choices and limitations of accountancy procedure, and therefore interpretation.

data is an interpretation of apparent facts

Whatever the accuracy or interpretation of these tangible bodily statistics, they have less to do with the measure of the emotive mind – your audience gaining positive perceptions about you through how you show, tell and do. This potential has previously been guessed at, if estimated at all, as an extension of the known data. The potential for joy or despair that these intangibles may signify is seldom reflected with any confident accuracy on any annual account. Instead, and until now, they have remained largely unaccounted for, or more usually, completely unknown. This is understandable, because these dynamics are elusive to the logic of arithmetic or traditional analysis. For this reason many do not attempt to focus or measure them at all, despite the disadvantages and risk this subjects them to.

Within the computer age we have become used to using terms such as hardware and software. Because society has learnt to accept and agree the usage of these two words, we can now readily communicate their difference and implication. They have, over time, become tangible enough for them to be used in this debate, for it can be clearly stated that hardware is an identifiable mechanical or physical item, a body, large or discreet but obvious nonetheless.

effective identity is mind over body

In contrast, the software, and its function, effect and potential value to the user, is far less easily defined. It exists in cyberspace, or call it what you will. Certainly a space which appears to defy physical boundaries. Yet software is a code or system written and therefore understandable by the human mind. As we did not author the human mind, we have a good deal more difficulty in understanding our own thoughts. Hence the ultimate intangible: the mind.

Your mind, our minds exist in a space and time unlike the more obvious physical world we appear to live within. We are both physical and emotional. Our bodies take up space, a space we can measure and agree upon, yet our imaginations escape all physical laws. Our thoughts fit within a framework which we have, over the centuries, struggled to build and understand. Concepts and theories only become tangible after consensus and, more usually, indisputable agreement. This agreement can take a long period of experience and post-rationalisation. The intangible may become at least semi-tangible as agreed by history. The intangible is the incomprehensible events of today, yet to be fully understood, yet to be agreed.

Valuing the 'mind' of an identity is acutely contentious. The cautious hesitate to agree with the more ambitious valuer, but all gamblers can at least find the comfort of common ground when agreeing tangibles. Therefore most data becomes a form of doomsday reporting; lust without intellect, the perverse priority to bodymap as though this particular body had not got a mind worth valuing. Such valuations account for body in historical and present terms, but cannot tell you who you are or the qualities your audience attributes to you.

True, tangible data – and limited data of opinion that is gathered by survey – can indicate the possible future, help you anticipate the probable and react in advance to your estimates of public opinion, earnings or market pressures. It can help you to establish sales, cash flow and other data-led forecasts, but data alone does not and cannot tell you the complete story. It cannot truly measure the dynamic values which your identity should be radiating, however hard it may try to do so. Unless we are more specific, no system on earth can measure quality, and indeed, arguably, no dictionary can give you a satisfactory or comprehensive explanation of the word. But it is within this battleground that fortunes are made or lost. You see what your rival cannot, then you worry as to whether their view may be more advantageous than yours.

Take a moment to contemplate Test 4 overleaf.

Test 4

Imagine you wish to produce and print a corporate brochure. The two separate statements below summarise the sales pitch of two potential print suppliers and their identities.

Print supplier A

WE OFFER YOU THE LATEST TECHNOLOGY.

Print supplier B

We offer you our expertise.

Consider that supplier A is majoring on selling tangibles, whilst supplier B is promoting intangibles.

The message to you is revealing in that it displays what they consider is the most important factor to both themselves and you, the potential customer. For these suppliers either statement may be correct. It depends, of course, on how accurately they perceive their market.

Now, considering the presentation of your identity, contemplate the following:

▌ What category does your audience most value about your organisation
    – tangibles or intangibles?

▌ Which order of importance would you prefer them to be placed in? To generalise and put it more bluntly, your identity and its presentation will offer one of the following three positions:

We offer you our mind

We offer you our body

We offer you a combination of both

A preference for tangibles, intangibles or an equal emphasis upon both is what your audience desires. Whether you elect to disagree or educate them otherwise, you would be advised to recognise their preferences. For some professions or organisations, the need to promote tangibles before intangibles will dominate. For example, your physical size, plant list, location, wealth, distribution, low prices or other attributes may be more compelling to your audience than attitudes, experience and values of character. Conversely, a list of tangibles may be much less important than you imagine, perhaps of no direct importance at all. So when telling an audience about yourself, don't make the mistake of getting these priorities wrong or you may only succeed in confusing, testing their patience or repelling them all together.

For example, it is not wise to spend the first three minutes of a five-minute presentation harping on about your geographical location and plant list if your listener is less interested in this (body) than your attitudes and level of service (mind). Likewise, avoid preaching about the quality of your mind when the punter is primarily interested in your body. You need not be entirely customer led. Often customers need leading more in the interests of the long term than immediate gratification, but you do need to ask what speaks loudest for you – organisation or individual: your bodily specifications or your less visible qualities and characteristics.

Effective identity is mind over body. Whatever the importance of the static tangibles, your visual identity should be designed to accentuate your emotive appeal, for it is the 'mind' of your identity which ultimately supersedes any other reality. It creates and bolsters the emotional perceptions of your audience. You need to explore this thoroughly enough to be able to recognise its valuable traits and promote them, or leave yourself exposed to the mercy of the unknown.

Recognition means the capability to manage, or else remain uncertain of creating and then maintaining an identity's direction and aim. Of course, the greater the distance your aim needs to travel and the more ambitious your objectives, the greater the need for a system of focus and calibration. You need to be able to focus the emotive content of your visual communications.

These dynamics are elusive of finite control, hence the endless debates about the true market worth of successful products and brands, yet they are the true destiny of an individual or organisation. They tend to endure, for better or worse. They create fortunes or destroy them. They instigate movement of desire or denial, action or inaction, advance or retreat. They are deeply rooted, usually by accident of birth or experience, and therefore difficult to identify, indeed often overlooked. How often do the successful fail to understand the underlying reasons for their success or the losers fail to remedy their fall from grace? And how often does the charismatic company leader become so entangled with the identity of their overall organisation or product identity that neither they, nor their audience, can manage to unravel the difference between the two? Such a strong leader can, unless managed otherwise, become confused with the identity and habitual values of the organisation or product, because the intangibles of the leader are deliberately used, or accidentally allowed, to dominate the intangibles of their organisation or product.

Unless you attempt to define the intangible mind which underwrites your identity you cannot manage its power and effectiveness. The values of what you do in terms of product and customer service may seem easier to identity. You provide a function and service that profits (benefits) your customers. Even so, there is a hidden, more emotive aspect of all that you do. In particular it is your visual appearance and the more emotive words you use to communicate your messages – what you show and do – that need to be tightly focused and under control.

You need to achieve this focus or you cannot knowingly lay the foundations of your identity. And if you cannot be certain of the foundations, you have serious cause to be apprehensive about the strength and stability of the structure you are intending to build. This takes insight and perseverance, but the reward is a certainty of success unachievable by any other means.

Firmwords

FOUNDATIONS

Your identity should be like a building constructed within the minds of those who encounter it and, in the same manner as any physical structure, capable of growing to a great height because of the strength of its foundations.

You cannot skip the foundation-building. You must budget for and produce adequate support. Instead of building upwards, you now find yourself digging downwards – and only to refill the holes later. This may test your nerve and patience: time appears to be against you and digging may not be the immediate satisfaction you desire. Meanwhile you may have the continual pressure of others peering over your shoulder. Added to which, before the earthmovers begin there may be a large amount of dangerous, awkward and sensitive demolition work to complete. It's not just concepts that stand in your way, but people too. These inconveniences must be negotiated before construction can begin.

if we must build on sand, let us know its quality

Whatever the current state of repair, and whether or not a complete rebuild is required, you must ensure the integrity of the foundations you are about to build on.

Before investing time and money in the pursuit of a new or improved identity, it is worthwhile contemplating how you will measure the relevance, effectiveness and accuracy of the work you are about to commence. This identity will be applied to many forms of communication materials and events.

Therefore a method of debate, selection and appraisal of the emotive content of these manifestations is not only invaluable but essential.

In deciding on your identity, are you planning a skyscraper or campsite? The foundations of the former need to support extreme weight. That much seems obvious. You may wonder how anything so large can stand so firmly rooted. The latter, like any temporary structure, perhaps an exhibition stand, appears at first glance to have a minimal requirement. But on second thoughts, if just one tent or caravan is one component of a much larger operation, and your overall target is still the stars, your identity will still benefit from skyscraper foundations. Of course a tent or caravan is portable, but their visual foundations should remain tuned to those of your core identity (your centre of operations) or, if you are a perpetual traveller, the strength of your back.

And how strong is your back? The location and building of foundations is hard work. Spade or mechanical digger, it is not for the impatient or those afraid to question themselves and others. The search is for the inherent materials that will be able to take the burden of weight and responsibility – and beyond just the initial launch period. The sooner you start, the better. Pity those who reach the first floor only to realise the foundations below now limit their planned growth.

If we must build on sand, let us know its quality. Your first unavoidable dilemma is to realise that it is the intangibles which are your foundations. Identifying and focusing these becomes the first priority of a sustainable identity. This means, for many, an uncomfortable level of abstraction. You need to identify what others may either not be able to see or not wish to risk being seen to see for fear of being foolish. The struggle to grasp what for many seems the unreachable takes you outside and beyond the normal confines of logic. Deny the validity of labelling these dynamics or not, we all are subject to them. Recall the tests at the beginning of this book and our tendency to make emotional judgements beyond any conscious reason.

your identity should be a zone of zero waste

These intangibles require descriptive labels. The need is for words that will not break too easily under the weight of inspection, words that inform and confer visual and emotive meaning. These words must pinpoint the heart of your identity when it is working at the peak of its focus

Illustration 8

The horizontal line is ground level.

What supports the visible must be of suitable strength.

*either your
identity is
growing or
it is dying –
there is no
in-between*

and potentiality. Not vagaries such as 'quality' or clichés such as 'leading edge'. These terms are too blunt or weak in substance and liable to misunderstanding or the arguments of fashion; such words are breakable in that they dissolve, fragment or subside, leaving behind alternatives that offer more visual clarity, character, resonance and durability. You need words of substance that will support weight and stress, concrete words that are capable of working tirelessly beneath the surface of your identity. For this reason, and because it is useful to refer to these words by name, they are called 'firmwords'.

MEASUREMENTS

Any fool can attempt to measure, but who can measure identity? The problem is that there is a need to measure. Without a system of value recognition, an identity can and will easily fall into disarray because it cannot be effectively managed or measured. An identity does not stand still. It cannot. It is active, growing by incremental gain and loss each day. It reacts and responds to the changes it must endure. It is both diminished and added to daily by the events and people who feed and support it, as well as those who draw sustenance from or possibly even attack it.

Disregarding the audiences outside the organisation, within it you may share common values and opinions about the desired identity, but unless the essence of those values can be translated and agreed readily, and with rapid consistency, the focus of the identity will stray.

An identity should be a zone of zero waste. There should be no wasted effort or needless expenditure of energy. Everything which emotionally or perceptually contributes towards the identity should exist for a positive and justifiable reason. In particular, all that you show and tell should be emotively focused. You can navigate this focus, and therefore make rapid decisions about what is valid and beneficial to the aims of your identity or not, by applying a simple guidance system: firmwords. For example, your management, staff or agency may, through ignorance or misinterpretation, contradict the intangibles

Illustration 9

unfocused identity	unfocused identity

consensus of identity through both structured and unstructured discussion with external consultants and differing levels of internal management on a project-by-project basis: ad hoc or improvised identity management

consensus of identity through the agreed use and debate of identifiable foundations and intangibles:

firmwords

unfocused identity	focused identity

Choose your method of identity management, and therefore focus.

*identity is
not a matter
of like or dislike*

upon which the identity is founded. And when presenting their vision for your identity – perhaps a new uniform or corporate brochure – what process of reasoning will you employ to measure the visual appearance and written content of their ideas? These ideas are threatening to add or detract from your identity. Unless you can instinctively and decisively challenge their inclusion, and with a consistent and unifying method of approval or rejection, you abdicate control. The emotive content and manner of your identity is under threat.

Identity is not simply a matter of style – like or dislike – for style alone may only be an embellishment, or passing fashion. The foundations of your identity should not be compromised. Their roots are your enduring strength and ultimate appeal. Therefore any aesthetic decisions should be consciously made with both these foundation values and your operational strategy objectives in mind. Everything else is a deviation.

If you fully realise the code of this focus, you can provide quick and incisive reasoning when judging any visual manifestation, from correct brochure design to correct clothing, from correct colour to correct shape.

So what words should be your firmwords? How can you find and describe in just a few single words that which denotes the underlying emotive appeal of your identity?

DESIGN CERTAINTY

Consider a possible firmword, 'interactive'. You might ask, does the identity it relates to, as well as the channels of media communication it uses, conform to the ethos of this word? Does the effect of such random elements as headlines, photographs and illustrations agree with, support and further clarify the meaning of this firmword, or do they contradict? Perhaps these elements do not imply, suggest or overtly state conformity or denial of this firmword. Perhaps these elements neither confirm nor refute, register nor suggest any connection, however tenuous, with 'interactive'. If so, the next and most obvious question is why are they being used at all? At best they may add nothing to the identity as indicated and measured by this single firmword. At worst they may detract, confuse or simply be a series of meaningless statements. If so, omitting them would be more advantageous than continuing to fund their use. And so the guidance of this one word – one I have only included here as a random example – begins to chisel an attitude of choice and control.

Of course, the precise relevance and rationale of a firmword depends upon the nature of the organisation or product it is intended to represent. For example, imagine that in this particular example, the firmword 'interactive' represents the notion of enabling users to communicate both into and out of an imaginary centre, regardless of geography, social or professional standing. It may represent reciprocality; to act on each other; to behave in a way that influences and responds to one another; a two-way flow of information, responding to input from the users and suppliers alike. 'Inter' could be interpreted as meaning amid; between; among; source; enter. 'Active' could be understood as given to action rather than speculation; practical; originating and communicating; working; effective; alive; and capable of modifying its state or characteristics in response to input or feedback. These details, the rationale behind a firmword, must be sufficiently established because this is the root of the root that supports and feeds all subsequent discussion and interpretation. Establish and know them well and the endless connections they provide will advance a mastery of identity unavailable by other means.

having 'design certainty' means a more appropriately creative as well as productive debate

These values should describe the combined effects of your visible identity. They are the vital messages and general style that your identity radiates, as created by your use of typefaces, photographs and illustrations. Their overall effect should be to convey and contain a worthy depth of meaning, which can stand debate within your own mind, as well as those in your immediate team. They should, within the realms of what must be a necessary abstraction, be wholly relevant both to you and your customers' needs, as well as being an active and simple recipe for creative decision-making and evaluation. Get it right and there is a big reward: design certainty.

You positively need a sense of design certainty. You need the ability to accurately channel the more emotive contributions of external designers and promoters, as well as internal management and marketing focus. This means an agreed understanding, partnership, knowledge and commitment, enough to give force and direction to all creative discussion and opinion, however unexpected, shocking or irrational those opinions may at first appear.

your aim should be to promote significant savings in time, anxiety and budget

The agreement of the foundations provides the rationale for all future discussions of this nature. What is considered to be correct or incorrect, in general terms or detail, will thereafter promote significant savings in time, anxiety and budget. The client stakes an ownership, understanding and involvement in their own identity, whilst the external designer, sharing the same agreement about the core and true nature of the identity's foundations, can unleash their creativity and commitment without hestitation but with a focus and confidence impossible to achieve by any other means. Complete knowledge of these values is far more likely to provide apt and exciting results than a designer fearful of a client's reactions to any given design approach or interpretation of brief. It is less worrying for the client too, because each presentation now has a basis of judgement to which all parties have agreed; uninformed likes and dislikes become easier to spot as being irrelevant, and positive or negative criticism becomes focused and more readily articulated. Designers can boldly challenge the client's understanding of what these foundations will bear, and the client can more intelligently participate in the creative debate of the design solutions being recommended.

DECIDING ON YOUR FIRMWORDS

You need to decide on your own firmwords. First, review your survey, where you gathered your thoughts and the thoughts of other interested parties. Look back at these notes afresh and spend some time further reflecting on the findings. Write down all the value headings relating to your organisation's service and ability, in the minds of your staff and your target audience. The values you are seeking should form a two-way mirror: that is, they should represent the fundamental strengths of your product or your service as well as being the chief motivators in the eyes and ears of your target audience. Simply scribble them all down for now without too much regard for where this is all leading.

Gradually, become aware of any similarities or grouping of words. Try to group all similar values together. At this early stage it may not be clear within each group which particular word is the strongest lynchpin. One word, or a word you have yet to identify will, by association, support the meaning of all others. That is, all the other words within this forming group can arguably be derived from this single source. In particular search for a key word that readily lends itself to visual and emotive interpretation: one that can be represented, conveyed and understood through the medium of pictures – in your mind, or via photograph or illustration. Depending on how obvious the link is between picture and word, it may require the support of some simple verbal or written qualification.

all graphics should be permeated with the same sense of meaning

This would also be true of almost any photograph or illustration used within the confines of an advertisement or other promotion, for seldom can a picture alone be used without a headline or other qualifying statement to make its purpose clear. (If it can, it is an icon, with a power beyond words, however many we may try to attribute to it.) The point is that the underlying statement of the pictures you are – from now onwards – going to be including in your identity communications is going to conform to, indeed promote, the essence of your firmword. More importantly, beyond the use of any photograph or illustration, the expert designer (a trained and visually literate person) can and should utilise the same word and meaning with varying degrees of subtlety or abstraction, so that all graphics such as layout, pictures and choice of typefaces, as well as all issues of format, headline and text matter, are permeated with the same general meaning. Firmwords are words which justify your existence as well as your message or communication. If you cannot justify an action or item of communication in relation to them, do not include them as part of your identity. No action is better than inappropriate action.

Test 5

To narrow down or formulate your firmwords, make three pin boards or desk surfaces under the three headings above.

Select and pin up all current visual manifestations of your identity onto one of the three pin boards making your selection on how you feel about them. Any item you feel uncertain about or do not identify strongly with as being either Positive or Negative must therefore be Neutral.

When judging any object such as buildings, vehicles, purpose-made exhibition stands, gift items, clothing or any other structures or methods of physical communication make selections on the basis of:
purpose – shape – format – size – weight – texture – colour

When judging actual content make selections on the basis of:
typeface – photograph – illustration – subject matter – word/phraseology – space – layout – colour

JUSTIFY OR DELETE

Be warned that from now onwards every visual and emotive aspect of your identity is going to have to justify its inclusion or continued existence by comparison with your eventually chosen firmwords. This covers all aspects of show, tell and do – and depending on the level of commitment necessary to achieve your commercial objectives, should depend an equal determination and tenacity in how you manage your identity.

To assist you in finding these words, don't just look at your survey notes. Unless it is a new identity for an entirely new venture, study all the current manifestations of your present identity. Study current usage of colours, typefaces, printed items, signage, photographic material, clothing, accessories and interiors with an eye for what most strikes you as effectively adding positive value to your progress in the marketplace, as well as that which is nothing more that ineffective or neutral. Also note any imagery that appears to detract from your identity.

Firstly, look for items which strike a major chord either in your heart or the hearts of others. These items may appear to be instinctively correct for the identity in question. They could be said to speak in a louder, more confident voice than the other items which surround them, as well as tending to positively increase the effectiveness of identity and your morale. Perhaps these items have already proven their effectiveness, and maybe this is already reflected in some measured increase in sales or market effectiveness. Also, perhaps a particular leaflet design, typeface or photograph appears, though you may not necessarily know why, to epitomise the ethos of the organisation or product being surveyed. Meanwhile other manifestations of your existing identity may only cause minor excitement, or none at all. Perhaps some may go as far as to embarrass or repel you.

If you are not sure of their contribution, then they are likely to be neutral elements of little use to you in the future. Other items may appear to be ineffectual or obstructive to the aims and objectives of the identity. This process does not mean reacting only to standards of workmanship or quality of printing but accounting for visual and emotive impression and empathy – you are searching for those items that either appear to improve you, deny you or else appear to do neither.

You may take your time and change your mind several times as you start to enter into this thought process. Your casual opinions should soon develop into the beginnings of a reasoned classification and understanding of what reflects your organisation in the best light. By now you should have three growing categories of material: positive, negative and neutral. You may still not have the links that bind or divide these categories, but the more you continue this progress the clearer these links – the commonalities of the good and the bad – will become. Refuse frustration until you begin to see an emerging set of truths.

Do not be alarmed if most of the items appear within the negative category or if, at this stage, you are not sure of the exact reasons for their initial selection. Notice that some items may contain contradictory elements: for example, you may feel a particular colour on a brochure is positive, even though the subject or style of an illustration appears to be negative. If one item needs dividing into two categories, simply get your scissors out!

Continue to make these instinctive divisions even if unsure of your reasoning. Trust your instincts! If you are short of elements to judge, complement by adding others. Borrow images or items from the brochures of others, magazines or other advertising material.

This process is defining patterns and profile. With the positive items only, gradually clarify your reasoning for each selection and the common denominators they share. Start to understand these common values and jot down randomly the words that best describe them as they occur to you. Add these to the values you have been scribbling down.

However unconvincing or baffling you find the beginnings of this process, group and regroup these words with the aim of amalgamating and reducing these groupings of value into as few as possible. You are defining several areas of concentration. Continue to puzzle the commonality between the words you are writing down in an effort to reduce the eventual number of groupings into three distinct groups. By striving for three groups of words you will ensure that your thoughts and the words themselves will receive thorough scrutiny.

No matter how difficult a task it may seem, reduce each group of words to just a single word. The aim is to distil your selection down to just a single word from each group – making three words in total. Yet again, this inevitably forces you to work extremely hard in justifying your selection.

To illuminate your search, make full use of a dictionary, thesaurus, synonyms and antonyms, or any other vocabulary tool. In particular, once you start to feel reasonably confident about a certain word, search for and compare other similar word meanings that perhaps offer slightly more energy or definition. There are likely to be several words fighting for the same position; allow yourself time and grace to prioritise them in order of effectiveness.

Once you feel near to completing this preliminary selection of three words, start to also notice the interaction between them. This should provide a further dynamic which none of the words acting individually is capable of achieving. Verify your selection by asking if each word accurately and steadily describes an element of what you and your organisation possess. Is it an authentic and (as far as possible) reasonably unique intangible that you offer? Is it – or could it possibly be – upheld in the opinions or desires of your audience? Are you are also confident of providing, defending and proceeding with this concept as part of your strategy for the foreseeable future? In other words, is each word justifiable? Your audience need never know these words. They remain code words of rude meaning, buffers of depth. They are your sanctuary and the emotive spring of your identity. They will support and justify your identity, rather than publicise themselves. We seldom see the foundations. Foundations support with an invisible ease.

now gain a new self-understanding of what is working and why

The words you are searching for need to relate to the visual and emotive aspects of your identity – both picture and word, show and tell. Continue to authenticate them against the items previously considered as adding to your identity. They should confirm or explain why these images appear to work so well. If you have the right words in your grasp the items you instinctively group together will now appear in a clearer light. You should begin to see a thorough revelation; a new self-understanding of what is working and why. Also test the words by applying them against the more obtuse visual manifestations relating to your identity, such as office furniture, automobiles and personal clothing. Being drawn from different groups, each word should promote a separate meaning and usage, lending each grouping a distinct visual interpretation. What is visually exploitable may be seen more readily by some, unappreciated by others. You need to be visually literate, or include a member in your team who can provide this insight. Ideally the designer you employ should be able to combine both visual and verbal insight, for it is this articulation of the gulf which often divides the two that is necessary if you are to fully realise and understand. Work together until you both understand the rationale of the firmwords. If they are imperfect, they are misleading and therefore inappropriate or possibly dangerous to use, so proceed with care. The upshot is that all members of your steering group should be able to understand and begin to articulate their application. What starts as a complex process of exploration should end in a simple clarity of language that all can begin to see the benefits of. When you are satisfied with your final selection, the words can be worthy of being called firmwords. 'Firm' because they represent the immovable foundations of your current identity.

Illustration 10

Here the same underlying word helps to support the other words and phrases – it is, in effect, their common denominator.

well-engineered

durable

thorough workmanship and materials

durable

traditional values

durable

When thinking about your own identity, work until you have found such a word capable of describing and supporting all others which would otherwise pretend to describe this one area of intangibles. In this example, 'durable' would appear to be suitable, and is a descriptive word capable of being translated and understood in both photographic images and attitude of word, speech and other presentation.

The result should be a visual definition of how your identity should be focused on both yourself and your audience.

Illustration 11

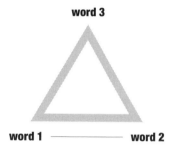

The final selection should ideally provide two words (words 1 and 2), which complement each other, but perhaps with some element of tension between them. It might seem as though these words have some contradictory effect upon each other. This apparent contradiction is a powerful signal that your selection is on the right path. The third word (word 3) presents itself as standing apart from the other two. It should reconcile the tension or contradiction between the other two.

These words become the mixture with which you will promote and measure the effectiveness of your identity. They may not directly refer to your literal business activity or product, indeed that is unlikely to be helpful. Instead, they are a combination that together create a consistent focus. They establish an emotive code for what is fully justifiable and in accordance with your identity and that which, however professional or attractive, is not.

Test 6

Below are some sample firmword combinations.
(word 1 – word 2 : word 3)

- geometry – art : active
- alone – communion : reprise
- change – secure : forever
- solo – family : happiness
- simple – intelligent : enlightening
- minimum – maximum : leading
- independence – teamwork : coordination

Each firmword combination can be applied to an individual, organisation, product or service.

Match each combination to one organisation, individual or product from the following list:

- technical authors
- laser and inkjet printers
- engineering software
- fashion house
- investment opportunity
- outdoor clothing
- internet service provider
- restaurant chain
- management consultants
- perfume house
- stockbrokers
- pop star
- laboratory equipment
- …this book

Firmwords form the foundation for endless creativity – and always within the boundaries of what fits and summarises your visual and emotive identity. Together they form a unit of multiplicity that maintains focus as well as provides the most direct route towards onward creativity.

Notice how unexpected and refreshing these combinations can prove when experimented with or swopped between one organisation/product and another. To the creative mind they offer endless ideas and image associations for focused show, tell and do.

Of course the definitions of each individual word and combination are personal to the organisation or product they belong to. Their precise meaning and justification may and should be known only to them. Unless you are fully versed in their character and management objectives, how else can you readily interpret their peculiar meaning and inference? What is clear is that you should develop a short, written rationale for each word and, in addition, the combined group of words as a whole, so that the interpretation and representation of the words can be further communicated, supported and explored as necessary.

USING FIRMWORDS

There is no limit to the useful application of firmwords. New updated combinations and subsets can be devised and employed to suit the complexity and depth of your identity. If chosen wisely, your firmwords are a simple and powerful reckoning tool for measuring the emotive focus of your identity – or for that matter, any article of communication which operates under the guises of your identity. Certainly use them when judging the effectiveness and relevance of such items as a logo, brochure, typeface, photograph, illustration, advertising campaign or office interior.

Gauge the validity of the concept and design by comparing them with your firmwords. An item may satisfy one or two of the three words, but does it satisfy all three? In such a way you can measure and, if you choose, score the performance of your identity communications. Traditionally Marketing only measures response to their communications, whereas with firmwords they can also measure this against conformity and focus of all outgoing messages. In other words, measure the focus of an exhibition stand and not merely the number of resultant sales leads. The 'success' of an exhibition depends on various factors, the actual exhibition stand design surely being one of the most significant. In such ways, Marketing can offer a further rationale to the productivity of their spend, and other board members more readily audit Marketing's validity in their efforts to focus and steer the organisation's ongoing identity. Such scoring matrices are easy to construct, as the following show, tell and do (STD) example demonstrates:

STD SCORING

Illustration 12

	Show	Tell	Do
Firmword 1	-1, 0 or 1	-1, 0 or 1	-1, 0 or 1
Firmword 2	-1, 0 or 1	-1, 0 or 1	-1, 0 or 1
Firmword 3	-1, 0 or 1	-1, 0 or 1	-1, 0 or 1

By scoring -1, 0 or 1 (negative, neutral or positive) you can grade a communication between the total extremes of ±9. Each of the nine categories marked can be supported by a coherent and easy-to-follow commentary in line with any officially sanctioned firmword documentation. In other words, there is an audit trail, and cause of redress, of interpretation and justification. Depending on the flexibility and need to manage, you may not need to score any of these items. A one-man band can be his own judge and jury. The point is that you have the choice.

Furthermore, if you have already determined which level of Critical 1, 2 or 3 each scored item corresponds with, you can produce a further weighting of scoring to reflect this, and develop a reasonably simple, yet highly revealing, series of measurements to suit your need to report and respond.

Test 7

With firmwords agreed, suitability of focus becomes both enjoyable and revealing. Consider the firmwords of **minimum – maximum : leading**. Without any other knowledge, contemplate what would be a suitable activity to sponsor from the list below:

- motor-racing

- croquet

- golf

- local school charity run

- cricket

- squash

- bar billiards

- tug of war contest

- beauty contest

- national televised song contest

- marathon running

- hunting event

- nature reserve

- drugs awareness campaign

- London to Sydney solo flight

Which activity satisfies as many of the three words as possible? Shun any which contradict any single firmword.

The quality and nature of the activities being organised and promoted, including those of the organiser, are both important influences. Start to eliminate, with harsh judgement, the subjects appearing to contradict, or not

*identify
the missing
ingredient*

fully or obviously satisfy, the notion of leadership. Some of the team games do include an element of leadership, but some focus upon a clearly defined leader more than others. The subjects also need to satisfy the notions of 'minimum' and 'maximum', so fail when compared with some of the others. 'Minimum' seems to infer distillation: the least possible, reduction, size or duration, certainly not waste or unnecessary luxury. 'Maximum' likewise seems to infer a certain rejection of compromise, as well as a full response, but also contradicts the word 'minimum' in suggestion of duration or size. 'Leadership' reconciles the other two words in that it can lead to both extremes, and often a worthy implication or combination of both.

For example, motor and cycle racing appear to offer both minimum and maximum – a power-to-weight ratio which strives for minimum weight and for maximum performance. Both produce leaders. Providing you are likely to be seen to support the eventual leader or facilitate the tournament, thereby making the selection of a leader possible, these would seem suitable.

The London to Sydney solo flight fails to provide a leader unless it contains an element which makes possible the breaking of a world record or other physical or spiritual barrier. Perhaps the aviator is already an established figure who represents leadership for other reasons. And so the arguments can continue. The important point is that the debate is purposeful and focused upon what is emotively correct for this particular identity. By establishing the incorrect so rapidly, we save unnecessary effort and expense, as well as protecting the identity by measurement and matching of values.

Through this trial and error of discussion you will gain an insight into what emotively benefits your identity and what, though professionally presented and not unappealing, is counter-productive or failing it. One of this technique's most instant rewards is the identification of the missing ingredient – a design is almost acceptable, yet 'something' is missing. Your firmwords should quickly prompt the correct answer.

As stated elsewhere in this book, there is a distinct liberation in concentrating upon what is correct and dispensing with all other effort. From now on you can repeat your aim with deadly accuracy. You can relax in the knowledge that all you do is promoting your identity in the direction you plan. This certainty of focus may significantly alter your attitudes to investment of time, money and other resources in general, impacting beyond the one third of your operation which is considered to be the domain of your identity alone. You can prioritise with a new alacrity and purpose, confident of your actions. What you now change, avoid or refuse will free you for the new opportunities before you! It is always a certain single-mindedness that best propels a clearly defined identity.

EXAMINING FAKE INTANGIBLES

if a hotel places a bust of Nero in its reception hall, it ought to know why

You should set about stripping away unqualified quantity in order to reveal pure and focused intention. For example, if you know the strength of a particular image, maybe a specific photograph that works well for you, why surround it with less effective imagery? If its positive contribution is at risk of being negated by some lesser images placed nearby, maybe you should think again. It is easy to water down or downgrade a presentation through presenting too much waffle.

The effective salesperson knows what not to show, tell or do. They never say too much. They know where to focus, and when to stop talking. The consistent quest for productivity is a vital driver to achieve competitive advantage. Why should your identity and its marketing be any less productive?

A fake intangible is the insincere or thoughtless use of signals or items that pretend to represent something the wearer does not fully intend, believe in or match with their own ability, intellect or moral intention.

If a hotel places a bust of Nero in its reception hall, it ought to know why, as a symbol or decoration, it is being used. Insincerity can be interpreted as foolish or insulting. In contrast, sincerity demands self-awareness and discipline – qualities prompted by proper adherence to firmwords.

The true and inherent are earned. You cannot simply copy the perceived intangibles of another and remain convincing. You need to experience your own truth through the labours of your own devotion. The spade before you cannot easily be handed to another.

Having successfully got this far, you can now proceed to plan the structure of your identity. What you build will be in accordance with the nature and strength of the firmwords. There are further decisions to make, but now the rewards for your early efforts will start to pay dividends.

Reality

FIRMWORDS IN ACTION

This chapter presents five real-life and successfully integrated identities, which for the purposes of this book should remain anonymous.

The object is to demonstrate the potential clarity and useful interpretation that can be gained when using firmwords as the basis for creative discussion. Each example is written in the style of guidelines to be followed by that organisation's creative staff and suppliers. Illustrations here are restricted to simple renditions of meaning, whereas more complete guidelines usually contain more company-specific graphics, such as logos, typefaces, layouts and colours – all explained and demonstrated as conforming to the firmwords being utilized. Later chapters show how firmwords translate into these other elements of identity.

Example 1, Organisation A

An online community and marketplace for the agricultural market

The focus of all this organisation's communications should demonstrate:

▍ Organisation A is not a member of the marketplace – it *is* the marketplace, central to the activities of its networks.

▍ Organisation A is an interactive service – which involves its users. Even though users may access Organisation A from remote locations, it should appear as a lively focal point populated and frequented by other interested and active users – all of whom are given the opportunity to gain greater, not lesser, involvement with each other and the wider day-to-day issues of the network and communities which they share.

▍ Organisation A has integrity. Organisation A's information services remain unbiased and all content should maintain authority, clarity and balance of viewpoint and debate.

It is useful to concentrate on three guiding firmwords that should, as far as possible, be the foundation of all Organisation A's communication materials – in terms of what is said, seen or read.

Central

Organisation A is 'central'. In this context, central means pertaining to the centre or middle; situated in; proceeding from; containing or constituting the centre of a market; and controlling all branches within that market from a common centre. Therefore an Organisation A network is central to the areas of interest which it serves.

Interactive

Organisation A is 'interactive'. It enables users to communicate both into and out of the centre (in most aspects regardless of geography, social or professional standing). It also stands for reciprocity; to act on each other; to behave in a way that influences and responds to one another; a two-way flow of information, responding to input from the users and suppliers alike. 'Inter' means amid; between; among; source; enter. 'Active' means given to action rather than speculation; practical;

originating and communicating; working; effective; alive; and capable of modifying its state or characteristics in response to input or feedback.

Balance

Organisation A is a provider of 'balanced' information. It selects and summarises this information in order to suit the needs of its users and the services being offered – a possible source of conflict which requires balance. Balance ensures trust. Users must trust the impartiality of the information presented and the channels of communication offered – including all information services, areas of e-commerce, product endorsements, etc – for if they did not trust this balance, they would be less inclined to use the services. In this context, balance means weighing up; poised freely on a pivotal central position; a regulation of information or system; a balance of justice, reason, opinion, action and principle; equilibrium – which means stability of forces within the system; and a general harmony of values, proportion and design. Therefore it is not unnecessarily antagonistic in statement, deed or appearance.

Evaluating communication materials by referring to these firmwords still leaves room for debate – and debate is healthy – the point is that an awareness of the importance of these values ensures that discussion remains focused. When designing or constructing any communication item, include as many of these values as possible. Communications without them – either directly employed or indirectly implied – at best will be ineffectual to the aims of Organisation A or, at worst, may be counterproductive or damaging to Organisation A's credibility and reputation. For example, consider the following headline:

Have access to the markets with Organisation A

As a headline, it is a statement only. It says, we are here – if you want us. It does not suggest any interactivity. It is rather lifeless. If users are seeking the benefit of interaction and a sense of community, this headline does not communicate this. Neither does it suggest any particular centrality – for will users expect to find all of the markets with Organisation A or only some segments? Also, if we consider 'balance' infers trust, a balancing of opinion, action as well as principle, this statement is arguably rather weak. Overall, it is straying from the firmwords, the underpinning values, that Organisation A should expect to be communicating.

Now compare that headline with the following:

Buying or selling – the current prices, online, now

Here, there is no mention of markets yet the fundamental basis of all markets is buying and selling – which is inescapably an interactive activity. 'Current' also infers both 'active' and 'central' – for this is the 'place' where it is currently happening – and users should be led to assume the central place – taking place live online as they deliberate whether to join in or not. The action of buying and selling implies the balance of the marketplace, and the rhythm of the sentence contains both a sense of balance as well as symmetry – though this is less relevant to our aims. Nonetheless, the overall result is more in harmony with the values of Organisation A and therefore much more effective in its strength and relevance of communication.

Illustrations and photographs should also be judged in the same way. For example, the following three images are two landscapes (which promote no interactivity), and an image of a telephone sales or support person, albeit active, but looking away from the camera – in other words, you the viewer. Rather than appearing central, these images appear remote. There is likely to be no pronounced exchange of valuable information and reaction between the images and the needs of Organisation A users.

Alternatively, the following three images are more in tune with Organisation A's values. The image on the left is a keyboard with a finger apparently making a selection – an interactive decision. The next image suggests a user in the field, again with some interaction: a mobile telephone. The third image is a telephone sales or support person, but this time fully engaged with the camera, in other words, you the viewer. There is a balance of tension, an engagement if you like, between you the viewer and the provocation that the images are intending to produce.

It is not often that a single image will be able to combine and project all three values together. However, what should be clear is that some images promote the desired values whilst others either do not, or oppose them.

Of course, the use of an image opposite to the firmword values you are attempting to convey, linked to another image or text which successfully retains correct values can be a useful ploy:

No change
Nothing happening
Not true
Organisation A

Example 2, Organisation B

A leading manufacturer of laboratory products

The mechanical specifications of the Organisation B identity obviously concern the mechanical elements of correct logo, colours, typefaces and typography.

Important as these are, they do not describe the emotional and perceptual values that should always underpin the products. These are the coded visual values that communicate Organisation B and its laboratory products at their best.

A product with an Organisation B logo does not necessarily qualify itself as an Organisation B product. A product must also demonstrate the correct values, and this can be achieved by using 'firmwords'.

In addition to their application to laboratory products, the firmwords as detailed here can also be applied to communication graphics, text and headlines, exhibition displays, promotional initiatives and sponsorships – in fact anything within the remit of Organisation B laboratory products and their promotion and distribution.
There are three laboratory products firmwords:

- **consistent**
- **unbiased**
- **discovery**

Organisation B laboratory products are consistent because they are durable, coherent, firm, solid and not contradictory in any respect – either in design styling or functionality.

Organisation B laboratory products are unbiased because they do not deviate, give bias to or prejudice the experiment or process.

Organisation B laboratory products represent and are used for the purposes of discovery.

Creative debate
The Organisation B laboratory product firmwords – consistent, unbiased, discovery – provide a method of dialogue and creative debate. Each word is representative of many things. Each definition can be added to, and a creative brief and solution can be argued against them.

If you are a designer, the first thing you may notice is that discovery, as a process, is not necessarily consistent. One can gently challenge the other, in so far as discovery can involve surprise – whereas to be consistent is to reduce or eradicate surprise. If someone is consistent in their behaviour, then they may also be considered predictable, and so on.

This tension and interplay between the two firmwords is intentional. The firmword that reconciles these two is the firmword unbiased. An Organisation B product does not suggest the answer to an experiment – instead its calibration makes the answer possible.

Consistent

To be consistent is to be in agreement; in harmony; in concordance; to be conforming; compatible and consistent with the facts. Consistent is never erratic, undependable, unstable or inconstant.

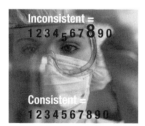

Inconsistent =
1 2 3 4 5 6 7 8 9 0

Consistent =
1 2 3 4 5 6 7 8 9 0

Unbiased

To be unbiased is to be objective; fair; impartial; non-partisan; unprejudiced; to be neither weighted one way or the other, but to be precisely true, adequate and accurate. To remain unbiased demonstrates purity, equality and a certain equilibrium. It is to remain balanced; it is the starting-point of pure; it is calibrated to zero. Unbiased is never to distort.

Unbiased:
1+1+1 = 3

Discovery

Discovery is to find; recognise; uncover; determine; ascertain; unearth; bring to light; originate; invent; and conceive ideas and developments. To discover can be a revelation; a journey or voyage of exploration. It is also monitoring for the purposes of detection; to make a transition or determine a course; to educate and to learn; and to be on the leading edge of progress. Discovery is never concealment or suppression.

Discovery

Example 3, Organisation C

A leading manufacturer of specialist vehicles

There are three Organisation C firmwords:

▊ **advancement**
▊ **orderly**
▊ **purposeful**

Understood and implemented wisely, they ensure the effective evaluation and communication of all that represents the Organisation C identity.

The central focus of all the Organisation C communications should demonstrate the following:

Organisation C advances

Advancement
To advance is to move or show movement in a direction of advantage; a pushing forwards which improves and contributes towards success, progress, development, and betterment.

It is not moving backwards, reversing, degradation, setback or decline.

Therefore any inference of decline, such as untidiness or disrepair, is a negative signal – because it infers the opposite to advanced, representing instead disorderly and unpurposeful.

To advance is a display of purpose. Organisation C enjoys both purpose and direction.

It seeks to advance itself and its customers forever forwards. Indeed, the whole notion of transport is to advance. Why else were wheels invented?

Organisation C advances with order

Orderly
In certain ways, the notion of being 'orderly' contradicts the word 'advanced'. This is because being orderly means avoiding the unexpected. Yet being advanced increases the chances of such accidents occurring – if only because advancement is achieved through experimentation.

Orderly is an adherence to tradition until a new technique, procedure or technology has been proven.

Organisation C advances by experimentation – but importantly only adopts the new ideas it proves as being advantageous to both itself and its customers.

Orderly is the discipline of the accepted; as stated, the proven. Organisation C is a proven organisation with proven methods and reputation. That this reputation also advances is made possible through the conduct and display of orderliness.

To be orderly signifies organisation, arrangement, grouping, systemisation, sequence. It is shipshape, tidy, arranged, methodical, harmonious and uniform.

It is not chaos, mess, sloppiness, topsy-turvy or untidy.

Organisation C advances with order and purpose

Purposeful
Intended, intentional, planned, deliberate, determined, resolute, affirmed, sure, certain, positive, definite, persistent, tenacious, unfailing, unfaltering.

It is not unintentional, inadvertent, offhand, casual, ambiguous, indefinite, vague, spineless, hesitant, faltering, wishy-washy or unresolved.

'Purposeful' means strength of purpose: this is the factor which reconciles advancement and orderly.

Strength of purpose makes the risk of advancement possible. It seeks order with justification, rather than the blind acceptance of procedure or habit.

It is objective. It is a target, aim, principle, point and rationale, plan, design, motive and motivation.

The purpose of Organisation C is equally purposeful:

▮ to be effective, not troublesome
▮ to keep its promises
▮ to act as an able partner
▮ to continually, and with purpose, advance its technical expertise.

Use the three firmwords – advancement, orderly, purposeful – as a means of measuring all components of the Organisation C identity.

This gives you the potential for 'design certainty'.

This is an identity where there is no wasteful or inappropriate marketing; no needless neutral or negative communications materials or activity; no unproductive discussion or argument about what measures up to the requirements and values of the identity.

Use these firmwords to brief, discuss and argue all visual manifestations of the identity including text and photographs. By understanding their import you can rapidly measure all which pretends or promises to communicate Organisation C at its best.

For example, when selecting the most suitable illustration the three following photographs appear very similar. Each depicts a road ahead. If forced to choose between them, the argument ought to include which is the most advanced.

Road 1
Any road could advance you, but this one appears less purposeful than either roads 2 and 3.

Road 2
Is it a road or a runway? It has a strong sense of order (the position in the road being firmly central), but the purpose and sense of advancement (without the addition of a suitable headline) is less clear.

Road 3
This picture achieves more than roads 1 or 2 because not only are we advancing, but an ordered and purposeful direction is implied.

1

2

3

Example 4, Organisation D

A PR and marketing communications company specialising in rural and countryside issues

There are three Organisation D firmwords:

- **inside**
- **outside**
- **growth**

Organisation D signposts and offers the inside – this is the inside sought by clients; the same inside where their messages are expected to be most efficiently heard, seen and accepted – and their interests, fears and rewards best served.

Organisation D also signifies the outside – for it understands and finely perceives the external issues to any given client situation. This is important because of the vantage, vision and depth of understanding this offers clients and their objectives. The subsequent ease with which Organisation D penetrates inside the target area of these objectives – indeed often helps to rewrite the brief – is all the more enhanced because of this ability to see from the outside in.

Organisation D offers unselfish growth – an ever-increasing productivity which it harnesses and focuses on its clients. Never seen to be self-serving, Organisation D's concentration is on fulfilling the aspirations and objectives of all client projects under its charge. It can be said that any significant and worthwhile growth benefits – if not demands – a heightened interaction and participation. The grown needs the grower and vice versa. Organisation D's attendance and attentiveness to any given 'communication problem' produces results consistently above average. This includes defending and countering barriers, difficulties and other threats to the objectives from wherever their source, client or external, in order to maintain the ultimate 'full bloom' objective of success.

The firmwords – inside, outside, growth – form the guide for the necessary and ongoing debate about what 'fits' Organisation D's identity and, therefore, what does not.

Whatever falls within the remit of the Organisation D identity – an advertising campaign, a dress code issue, a decision on sponsorship, an office interior project or any other visual manifestation of the identity – should be briefed, discussed and judged from this common fulcrum.

It must be acknowledged that an identity is a living culture. It is never static. It is added to or subtracted from on a continual basis of incremental change and advance. It is a process with which we must take great care, as it evolves with or without our guidance and stewardship – 'with' obviously being preferable! This because if we do not seek to guide and measure, we stand no chance of managing one of the cornerstones of our present and future success.

Here are some more detailed justifications:

Inside

Inside means the inner part of whatever subject we are discussing; the inward thought or meaning. It is interior; centre; core; middle and heart of the matter. It is generally, though not necessarily, the centre of any given field. True, this can also equate to favoured, advantaged and exclusive, in so far as an Organisation D client hopefully obtains all of these things. But it is also a clearly seen

Inside can be represented in many different ways: inside the machine; included in the meeting; the surprise of gaining inside; the contentment of inside; inside knowledge; inside or 'getting in' the media; gaining the inside line – making inroads to personal or corporate advancement.

entrance – for the majority of would-be clients who see it an open door leading to what lies beyond their present circumstances. It is (with a few exceptions, such as conflict of client, or the occasional journalist who wants to know too much) inclusion for all those who elect and choose to be included. Exclusion, where it occurs (and on occasion it must), is never insensitive or impolite – for manners should always remain impeccable, as befitting the ease and certainty of those who hold the ticket for the centre court. So it is exclusive, but not so exclusive as to be labelled clandestine. At times it is necessarily confidential and private, but never inappropriately so. It is the 'inside' that clients seek, or at least the castle gate to the inside they believe lies beyond.

Inside also represents insight: penetration of perception; the intent of sensitivity; perspicacity; acuteness; acumen; the seeking of information to attain deeper understanding; judgement; comprehension and vision. It is never insensitivity, dullness, bad judgement or tunnel vision.

To gain the inside means getting into, or through, the barriers that might normally prevent us; to gain entrance; to affect deeply and touch emotionally. Odd as the word may seem, 'emotionally' is mentioned because what we do is, if we do it well enough, stirring and, possibly for some observers, profound. Organisation D's inside is above the average point others may otherwise expect. So a refusal to accept the

acceptable has a part to play in the mantra. Organisation D pushes the boundaries and abilities of its clients in order to gain them the inside they deserve.

Outside

When discussing 'inside' it helps to define it by comparison to certain aspects of 'outside' – such as matters of inclusion and exclusion. However, in relation to Organisation D's visual identity, outside has other points of significance...

Certainly a great deal of Organisation D's activities concern the biggest outside of them all: out-of-doors. But outside can also mean outside oneself. Organisation D facilitates this advantage: it promises to extend the physical and mental boundaries of those 'unOrganisation D'. It introduces the possibility of situations elsewhere: external or beyond the limits of one's presently perceived sphere of interest or activity.

At its most obvious, outside is a picture of an open field – the world outside buildings and their confines. Yet it helps if this outside is displayed with further meanings attached to it other than representing out-of-doors.

Outside wanting in.

The sheer beauty of a landscape may be defendable, but a combination of 'inside' or 'growth' makes any image of outside more potent still.

'Outsider' is also a useful source of imagery: the non-assuming or non-aware consumers; those who do not belong to your circle but are either victims, beneficiaries, or perhaps potential customers/end-users.

In general, and let us not forget, Organisation D is expected to continually hold a vision and perception of the external but related issues. It is this outside – the outside of brief – which had it been spotted earlier by the client would have either solved the brief or been rightly included from the beginning. It is this version of 'outside' that constitutes one of Organisation D's most crucial competitive advantages.

Growth

The development; the evolution; the evolvement; the cultivation; the nurturing; the increase; the expansion; the broadening; the extension; the enlargement and flowering.

Organisation D advances through growth – in particular, through the growth of its clients.

Growth does not always mean unfettered proliferation and physical expansion – for growth can take many less visible forms. It can be an improvement of mind or corporate body; the rise and progress sought, discovered and employed. It can be a sense of fullness and fulfilment; completeness; thoroughness; realisation; implementation and accomplishment.

Growth can often be measured, implied, witnessed or gained through the transfer of knowledge.

Example 5, Organisation E

An engineering software consultancy

There are three Organisation E firmwords:

- **automatic**
- **interference**
- **knowing**

Automatic

Automatic means out-of-sight out-of-mind – automation, by its own nature, both necessary and working by itself without any direct human intervention. Automation saves mental and manual labour. It proceeds unaltered unless we intervene.

Automatic are the patterns that whilst we see, show and debate, others may not 'see' without the expert guidance of Organisation E.

The visual inference is always that a process is at work, and further, that it is at work on our behalf. It has been set in train deliberately – it is *not* an image of being deeply meaningless, such as a wholly abstract image with no sufficiently obvious repeating form, as shown below. Here the pattern possibly suggested by the 'second' cloud might hint of a process developing, but it is far too weak by itself to remain credible.

Even so, clouds, clichéd and deeply meaningless graphics though they so often are – and it is a good idea to avoid using them because of that – can be adapted to serve the firmwords of Organisation E:

The visual opposite to any firmword can be used effectively as a deliberate counterpoint to a second message, providing that second message conforms to the original firmword(s). For example, use an appropriate headline or else use a repeating pattern to create a suggestion of Automatic.

Self-contained?

It could be a good idea

It could be a bad idea

Automatic also represents the potential for something more profound or penetrating than its surface may indicate. This is because any automation contains levels of operation and complexity hidden from view. To see and understand you need either the knowledge of the expert or – and wouldn't it be useful – some x-ray specs.

Therefore when showing photographs of process plant it is a good idea to show these in negative (reverse reading) so as to indicate that Organisation E is entirely aware and concerned with what often cannot so easily be seen – the invisible which produces the effect of the visible – the more obvious surface our more ordinary experience is subjected to.

A further aspect of automatic to be understood is that of something bigger and more complex than merely what we see before us. This particular automatic, this automation, gives rise to the impression that it has its beginnings before the point where we find ourselves viewing its progress and also continues beyond this point of current viewing.

Interference

The second firmword is a positive interference. This is the point when, with full awareness and judgement, someone is seen to alter the course of a process or automation that would have otherwise proceeded along its predestined path. Without this executed intervention, the automation being interfered with would have continued on its planned path.

A precise intervention in an environment strongly automatic.

Shall you tell him or I? Interference – positive and necessary, whatever the short-term consequences.

The reason for this type of interference is to further action, give momentum to, fix, alter, change direction of, snapshot or take personal and absolute charge of the situation. It is a moment of personal power – power exercised because the automation being interfered with needs feeding or harvesting.

Interference is a form of disruption – but always a positive and clearly understood one. It is not an uncertain interjection of worsening confusion. It is always acute.

Knowing

If automatic is the laborious result of past actions and experiences, then interference is the ability to dip into or ride upon that source of energy. It is that still, self-conscious and transformational moment of knowing when and what you do matters most. It is that contained and pivotal moment of balance when you hold the scales, and the world revolves or changes direction because of you.

Knowing is the reconciling force between automatic and its opposition, interference. It is the intellectually precise and critical moment of choice and decision, the exact knowing moment between observing automatic and allowing it to continue uninterrupted, or to intervene, adjust or perhaps test the result. It is a balance of judgement – discretion, discernment, prudence, wisdom, clear-headedness, perception, perspicuousness, acumen, intelligence and understanding. It is a self-knowledge, profound – and never a struggle, or act of conceit. It is not seeking, rather it is knowing what is. It is perception of the moment.

It punches beyond mere determination, opinion and seeking. It is beyond the not unworthy ability to weigh, estimate, ponder, consider, deliberate, assess, compare and evaluate. It is knowing the answer, but more, knowing perfectly within the moment.

A specific and well-intended intervention. Knowing eyes also meet the camera lens.

1 I'll try this   2 suddenly unsure   3 still unsure   4 but I'll try again

9 I'll try this   10 I'll try this   11 what next?   12 I'll try this

17 now I'm frustrated   18 now distracted   19 now puzzled   20 or is it him puzzling me?

25 and now I'm on full alert   26 but all this waiting   27 and more waiting   28 I've got an idea

33 but that didn't work   34 but now I get it   35 and this will hit the target   36 my time is here

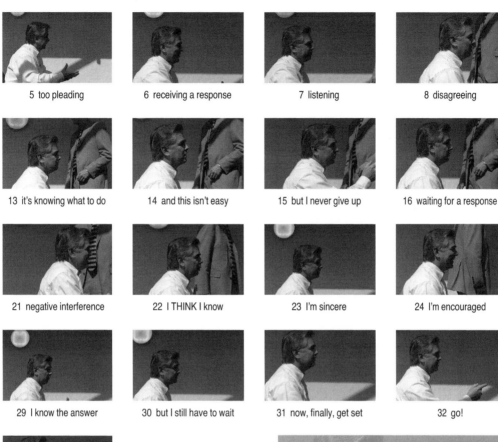

5 too pleading

6 receiving a response

7 listening

8 disagreeing

13 it's knowing what to do

14 and this isn't easy

15 but I never give up

16 waiting for a response

21 negative interference

22 I THINK I know

23 I'm sincere

24 I'm encouraged

29 I know the answer

30 but I still have to wait

31 now, finally, get set

32 go!

37 perfect knowing

Automatic, responsive, aware, intent and following through without hesitation. To his audience his actions are a positive interference, the result of a perfectly balanced, seamless and spontaneous mix of knowing – this conforms to and is Organisation E projecting at its most potent.

The section of the photograph cropped accentuates the impact and concentration of firmword values.

Automated to the hilt, the interference is his
to give and receive. He is in control. After all it
is his choice to walk as he works. And with all
that baggage, a sense of knowing what is and
matters mosts – physically and emotionally – will
not go amiss.

Style

SETTING THE RIGHT TONE

You need to fine tune how you distribute your identity and message, because the manner and tone of your presentation go a long way towards determining how common or rarified, elitist or commercial you are judged to be. Are you a nonentity, a cult, a regular cool dude, or a mainstream extravaganza? Are

are you a cool dude or a mainstream extravaganza?

you the struggling artist working outside the current mainstream, whose success is likely to be posthumous? Are you consciously on the fringes of the main market for reasons of integrity, insecurity or vision? Is this position uncomfortably ahead or behind the current market? Alternatively are you so bang in the gravitational centre of a collapsing marketplace that its fate is about to be yours? Strange as this may seem, is your current market success compromising your future?

You cannot always choose how close to the market centre you orbit, but you still have brakes and steering, however ineffective in the face of some market forces. One major, but crude identity control is how much should the identity be seen to advertise and sell? The more difficult markets to sell into are those where minimal or covert, rather than overt and more aggressive, promotion is demanded. All identities need to advertise but you must choose how obviously you are seen to do so – all of which concerns your key average of distribution.

BUILDING CHARACTER

Just as we are able to perceive the personality of the individual, the character of an organisation or product is very real.

Character is perceived through the experience of our senses. As we hear, touch, taste, see and smell we estimate and formulate our opinion. The greater the number of senses engaged, the more influential the experience. Each sense interprets all manner of verifiable or implied information. For example, you can hear whether someone is loud, but you can also 'see' loudness by the implication of other signals such as vibrant colour or forceful action. Arguably, the strongest sense is what we see, and, as argued at the beginning of this book, we all tend to believe what we see. This general truth can now be developed for, to a lesser or greater extent, we also believe what we hear, touch, taste or smell. Such limitations make us human.

So an identity can appear loud or retiring, passive or assertive. It can create the impression of youthfulness, maturity, antiquity, impertinence, humour, seriousness, calmness, an activity or energy level of any sort, or any other combination of characteristics you choose to communicate by design, or hit upon by accident. These issues are issues of interaction. They are about how your identity connects to or involves the audience.

UPPING THE PASSION

How much passion does your identity involve your audience in beyond their likely preferences? For example, a vehicle is a mode of transport. For some this means a desire for function, for others an acceptable combination of function and passion, and for a lesser minority passion at any price, including unreliability and inconvenience. The addition of a conservative, flamboyant or outrageous colour, shape, noise or other aspect of design needs to be defended as being within the realms of personality that it is your intention to project. In extreme cases, such as the classic car, the product may even go so far as to involve the user in its intrinsic fragility or unreliability, provided the user is forgiving or indulgent enough to appreciate this excess of personality. In other words, passion or romance is one of life's more irrational motivations, and it is this element of needing or expecting more than just the rational that we seek to justify in so many of our choices and purchases.

Where the application of passion is appropriate it may work wonders, glossing over otherwise unforgivable features or consequences. Elsewhere it renders the organisation or product inappropriate, unacceptable or distasteful.

Dressing an identity with too much hype is a mistake when its inherent exclusivity and desirability (its above-averages) mean it will be in demand anyway. Better that it be sought after or requested rather than 'sold', prostituted, offered or promoted too freely. This is also about judging both the dignity and distance you wish to set between your identity and the wider spread of the market. The design details of your visual identity, such as colour, shape, size and space issues, will significantly form your perceived character.

Consider the graphics you choose for a logo. In broad terms, all design falls into one of two categories: classic or romantic.

Classic graphics are those defendable by straightforward reason. They may literally represent your marketplace, category and product. They don't contain any real surprise or major pretence. They do not seek to divert or deceive the audience away from the true or literal nature of the product. At most, they provide a low level of shock to an audience and do not overtly challenge them or their expectations. This is the recipe for being traditional (with a tendency to be seen as old-fashioned), placing you at a predetermined distance behind or outside current fashions, time or mode. Alternatively, to position yourself exactly on or slightly behind the leading edge of fashion usually translates as 'smart' – until market movement begins to leave you behind, as it inevitably does. Frequent review of an identity will keep it relevant to the changing position of the current market, just as some confectionery products, despite their market launch several decades ago, repeatedly adjust their identity to prevent aging.

decide on a category of classic or romantic

If classic graphics are fairly easily assimilated by your intended audience, then romantic graphics are a break with the expected. They contain a shock value which promotes a concept of newness, such as the new philosophy, theory or practice, and, of course, the controversial. These graphics build an element of risk into an identity and present you with a problem, for they will test the audience's grip of reality. Such graphics are abstract – often a metaphor – and sometimes actually meaningless. They attempt to invade the audience's emotional need for indulgence or dreaming. They can often work through a connection which disrupts previous expectations; or an exploitation or coincidental connection between two formally unconnected elements that appear to form a new truth; a wishful idea, story or emotion; a transformation, journey or movement; an escape or apparent removal of otherwise real boundaries; or, in general, an emphasised or exaggerated plea and use of fantasy which creates an identity beyond the truth of the individual, product or organisation's reality.

surprise can excite in both directions

Your willingness to change, alter or reinvent reality, and use a level of fantasy which you feel to be beneficial, acceptable and sustainable for the time necessary to serve your objectives, should be carefully discussed and decided upon as part of your brief to yourself and your designer.

Presenting an identity that attempts to transform or lead an audience in a direction other than they previously intended is a surprise; and surprise produces reaction, which, if carefully thought through and implemented, can produce spectacular and positive results. But surprise can excite in both directions – a polarisation that can just as easily stun your audience into inaction as action, define taste or create distaste, liberate or threaten insecurity, create or destroy prejudice, validate or outlaw, attract or repel.

Much as you might seek it, instant attraction is not always a good thing. The suitability, appeal, cleverness and humour that a logo or logotype suggests must be appealing enough to succeed when first encountered, yet endure and hopefully extend its appeal over several years.

A design should not necessarily satisfy your appetite and reveal its entire content too soon. The most successful designs radiate their energy and engage you over a longer timespan. Their initial impact may be deliberately ordered, and often simplified, in order to ensure the desired longevity. The old adage of 'less is more' is so often proved true. A designer presenting a simple idea should be given the grace and time to allow the design to work upon you.

Don't be guided solely by your preliminary reactions to the presentation of the idea – for if presented to you by a designer, be aware that this is an introduction untypical if not impossible for your eventual audience. They will not and cannot share the same experience as you. Your approach, relationship with your designer, responsibility and attitudes towards risk and fear cannot be theirs. Instead, however favourably or otherwise you may feel about the presentation, I recommend that you spend a minimum honeymoon period of three days to fall in or out of love with any significant design or creative proposal. Be sure to build time into your schedules to accommodate such periods of reflection.

CULTURE

You cannot escape yourself. You have culture. Not necessarily one of appeal or relevance to your audience, though you may hope so, but the culmination of your evolution. To a large extent, regardless of how you present yourself, this culture will remain visible, a display of self, for better or worse, which cannot easily be disguised or ignored. To date, it comprises your journey of finding, advancement and failure. It is the history of your quest to fulfil the potential you believe is both necessary and possible. It is your present truth, regardless of any identity you choose to dress over it.

Geographical culture affects and effects us all. It can only be our 'perception' of area and nationality, because these forms of culture, regardless of our experiences, cannot be defined by any set of absolute laws, but are a random series of generalisations. These may be considered inaccurate and at variance with the viewpoints between the observer and the observed. Seldom will either share or agree the same viewpoint. What you may understand to be the geographical or national traits of your neighbour may to them seem inexplicable, irrelevant or downright laughable.

Culture is a always a form of pretence. It pretends to be itself, at times may even parody itself. Your culture is also the full gamut of association you allow yourself to reside within – not necessarily what you say but how you say it – not necessarily what you wear but how you wear it. And so it permeates you. In particular beware your national culture, for it can dominate the parliament of your mind

culture is always a form of pretence

133

without conscious election. This understanding is important if you are sailing into alien cultures: the immersed rocks of the culture you are entering into, and the danger that your culture may inadvertently clash with theirs.

LOST IN TRANSLATION

Understanding an organisation's culture, like another person's identity, is a process of decoding. Its visual identity (corporate identity) tells you one set of messages, whilst its culture of behaviour affirms or denies this. The reception interior and the logo say one thing, the dress and mannerisms of the receptionist say another; its marketing literature promotes it as a competent business but its external and internal signage system indicates the reverse.

When a client or supplier arrives at your premises, how must they judge you? How easily will they have followed your directions; found the correct parking place; located the correct entrance; opened the door the right way; felt comfortable with the procedure for entering the building further and judged the greeting they receive? If you are expecting them to wait in a reception area, in what circumstances must they wait and, whilst they do so, what visual, verbal and behavioural messages are you offering them with regard to your taste, manners and integrity? This is the 'truth' you present them with. They might endure this before meeting you for the business transaction that you have otherwise perhaps so meticulously planned.

you don't need to know the rules of tennis to enjoy watching the game – but it helps

Think about how your audience must work in order to reach the judgement you want them to make about your organisation. The labour required and its benefits require a decision, an inevitable decision. Your culture or the language of your organisation stands in the way. Easy or difficult, it may require no initial understanding or else significant preparation, training and prior knowledge. The energy, ability and inquisitiveness of your audience will vary. These are the barriers which culture can present and which either enhance or inhibit the effectiveness of your corporate identity. If your culture persistently confuses or contradicts itself, then the time needed for decoding – and reaching a situation of trust – extends accordingly. Ultimately, how soon does your audience 'get it'?

Does your presentation confuse your audience to the point where they would rather make a glib judgement of apparent value than be inclined to enquire any further?

False judgement may be the judgement of convenience: you wore the audience's patience down. They gave up part way through the maze you set before them. The obstruction they grew frustrated with came to be seen as your truth. Beware, for it is the involuntary signals and mannerisms that reveal this inner character. And your audience is watching. Their assumptions about you may be that your apparently natural or unplanned appearance and behaviour is not only more fascinating than the formal message or display you are offering them, but more likely to prove a reliable and accurate estimation of your true identity.

Behavioural culture forms a large part of your identity – the part you may not have questioned enough. A common attitude is to defend yourself and your present systems without compromise, expecting others to adhere or succumb to your culture, whether this is actually profitable or not.

In all areas of show and tell it is what you don't say that speaks the loudest. Your involuntary signals are treated as genuine. The spontaneous, the improvised are believed. This can be actual or rehearsed. Alternatively, pedantry advertised to the point of tedium can also prove to be a benefit. For example, an engineer who proudly claims to leave nothing to chance won't dazzle you with personality, but otherwise knowingly communicates his own version of thoroughness.

Illustration 13

Involuntary signals speak the loudest.

*are you master,
servant or first
amongst equals?*

How deeply you are concerned about the depth of your identity determines how life-changing your identity will become. Intelligent management recognises it as a vehicle for meaningful change and advancement. Identity can be the precursor and justification for excellence. Effective identity produces energy, motivation and movement – reorganisation, savings and reward. Identity should be the best investment you have ever made; if it proves otherwise, something is seriously wrong.

Generally it is best to approach your audience as equal to equal, and dress accordingly. How you do this should be in line with the power status your audience prefers. We all tend to form expectations about the status of those we encounter, whether assessing by appearances alone or other more complete information, and these expectations demand to be affirmed or denied as quickly as possible.

But do not be afraid to upturn convention. Like your audience, your own culture grew up around your feet because of your environment, circumstances, guidance and inherent character, or else was assimilated from others, perhaps without question, during a formative period of your development. Other culture may have been adopted through insecurity or fear – the culture of those you once considered to be competition, threat, idol or peer group. So you walked their walk, talked their talk.

Culture, natural or pretending to be, should enhance and add value to your identity. For example, interiors and costumes should further promote the values of your identity. They should never be considered irrelevant, because this display of culture supports the humanistic side of an identity where personality or personnel meet an audience. Where audience security is paramount, as for flight staff, police or security personnel, culture of environment, dress and conduct become elements especially vital to effective communication.

DOMINATION

When thinking about your own identity, do you seek to dominate your audience, interact or disappear amongst them?

Illustration 14

middle ground

Who dominates whom – your identity or the identity of your audience?
If you meet halfway, what is to be judged the halfway point?

DRESS SENSE

If an identity structure is the framework, what dress sense do you decorate this framework with? How you 'dress' your identity structure reflects your awareness of etiquette. Personality, or certainly an excess of it, can undermine an identity if it is not contained within a suitable framework of expression. In other words, it needs to be neatly ringfenced, so it may freely occur only within well-defined areas.

For example, some markets may demand formal dress, such as traditionally tailored suits, but the wearers can still express a glimpse of their personality through their choice of dress accessories. In the same manner a tactical military

Illustration 15

Letterforms are the most important and essential means of conveying verbal information. They also carry emotional and aesthetic information which impacts on how the verbal message is read.

Letterforms are the most important and essential means of conveying verbal information. They also carry emotional and aesthetic information which impacts on how the verbal message is read.

Letterforms are the most important and essential means of conveying verbal information. They also carry emotional and aesthetic information which impacts on how the verbal message is read.

Letterforms are the most important and essential means of conveying verbal information. They also carry emotional and aesthetic information which impacts on how the verbal message is read.

Letterforms are the most important and essential means of conveying verbal information. They also carry emotional and aesthetic information which impacts on how the verbal message is read.

Letterforms are the most important and essential means of conveying verbal information. They also carry emotional and aesthetic information which impacts on how the verbal message is read.

Letterforms are the most important and essential means of conveying verbal information. They also carry emotional and aesthetic information which impacts on how the verbal message is read.

Letterforms are the most important and essential means of conveying verbal information. They also carry emotional and aesthetic information which impacts on how the verbal message is read.

Each typeface creates and conveys different emotional and aesthetic information.

aircraft can express the personality of its aircrew within a limited display area, perhaps allowing for a small personal illustration or motif. Within such clearly demarcated areas, these flashes of personality can be as individualistic as is wished. Because they are countered and strictly surrounded by the order of the overall identity, and clearly seen to be so, they can be understood, tolerated and expected. They do not challenge the overall identity structure.

These examples of containing personality merely make the point that dress sense, in its broadest sense, means dressing for the occasion. There are both casual and formal situations and markets within which an identity must necessarily operate. Some promotional work may demand a more relaxed attitude or indication of casual style. Some items, such as a 'fun pack' designed to appeal to child passengers on an airline, obviously need to communicate at child level, yet also still appear to be belonging to and authorised by the overall identity. Therefore an amusing or informal approach may be appreciated by all, adults and children alike.

But should this same air carrier allow its aircraft livery to dress down too far, it may challenge its audience's notion of occasion as well as structure. Formality relates in part to preparation and seriousness. The preparation of aircraft for safe flight is a highly regulated procedure. Therefore, if the codes of pattern appear to challenge this necessary sense of strictness and formality through the use of excessively casual graphics, or inappropriate pattern repeats, the result may contradict audience drivers. You may make them feel insecure.

The point is that dress sense should be correctly applied and managed, however spontaneous it may occasionally need to appear. Your dress code must work within the structure of your identity. It should positively confirm your purpose and value.

VOICE

Typefaces are your written voice. Different typefaces imply different character, and tone, regardless of the content of your words. The best typography has grace and a certain invisibility: in other words it does not upstage the message being presented, but rather is a successful conduit through which the message is imparted, and with as little unsuitably false or negative bias as possible.

Some typefaces more than others exert a strong identity in their own right. A few become permanently associated with particular organisations or products. Indeed, many organisations operate with their own unique typeface – a font and font family cut especially for their usage. Owning the copyright has many advantages: in theory they have a typeface designed to exactly fit their personal requirements, and one which, through use, may be uniquely associated with their identity.

The distinction between one typeface and another may be due to subtleties of design too slight for most to notice or consciously care about. But the visual effect of one in relation to another becomes more obvious when comparing them side by side. A fast and effective way to judge the influence of a typeface to be used in text, therefore, is to compare it with blocks of other faces, as illustrated overleaf in Illustration 15. The overall effect is to reveal more of its visual traits.

PITCH

Forgetting technical terms of differentiation, which determine one type style from another, typefaces can be swept into several broad categories. These can include fat, thin, squeezed, expanded, ornate, austere, clinical, humorous, serious, dull, bulky, readable and unreadable (dependent upon proportions and weight), as well as any other attitude, mood or pretence one wishes to name. Some shout, some whisper. Some are upmarket, others downmarket. Some have vintage, allude to a period of history or other association. Some are friendly, others foreboding. Select and experiment on the basis of decoration, weight and, finally, the shape of any key letters or characters within the names of the identity you are constructing.

A group of typefaces within the same style can be referred to as a type family. A collection or combination from different families is a combination. Family or combination, if this group is to speak as a team, in unison, by contrast or complement, you must select the fonts with care. Also, space the typefaces with equal attention to detail, for the set (the space between characters) or leading (the space between each line) can radically alter the appearance of the same font.

The process of selecting the correct fonts for your identity is one of referring to your firmwords. Certainly the majority of typefaces will be an unsuitable match for your identity. Insist on finding the perfect combination of typefaces for the task in hand.

Illustration 16

hello!

hello

hello hello!

hello

hello

Every typeface is a voice of personality.

COLOUR

Everything within our world displays itself by the use of colour. Even apparent black and white. In tone, texture, light and shade, natural colours, both iridescent and delicate in tone, surround us. These colours of the natural world appear to have reason or purpose – and certainly beauty. Likewise, the colours you use for an identity should have similar reason, purpose and empathy with the objectives of your identity. In particular, note the divide between naturally derived colours (colours of history and harmony) and more modern derivatives, and decide the basic direction of your colour palettes. It is unwise to mix the two, unless you have justifiable reason to turn history on its head.

Colour is emotive. It represents many values, including age. One day it may be proved that colours can heal us. For every graduation from the light of day to the dark of night – from white to black and every tone between – colour signals the season and time of day. So if you are promoting the English Breakfast, evening colours are out! Colours can pinpoint precise periods of history: a particular year, decade or century. Many colours available today were not obtainable in the past. Invention and advances in colour technology have greatly expanded the range of colours available, as well as the material upon which they can be successfully reproduced. This expansion and availability of colour has changed our perceptions and usage. For example, the colour white has changed as technology has advanced. Formerly a vellum or creamy consistency, modern whites are capable of much greater brightness. For this reason the apparent age, and therefore tone of white (or any other colour) used on behalf of an identity should be chosen with care, or else run the risk of contradicting the time values of the identity.

justify the colours you use

The vitality of bright colours tends to suggest youth and an optimism towards the future, whilst darker tones often appear to indicate maturity and values established in the past.

Pastels, an alternative to bright or sombre colours, by their softness of tone, blur the boundaries of age and gender. Compared to 'solid' colours, they appear gentle, yet indefinite. This may suit some applications but be positively wrong in others. You wouldn't think much of pastel road signs. Or, put it this way, you might, but would others take them seriously?

Fashion is also a major factor when selecting colours. Certain tones, with only occasional slight variations, remain fashionable over very long periods, whilst others arrive like shooting stars, vividly announcing themselves overnight only to burn out just as quickly. Whilst they remain in vogue it seems that such colours can do no wrong, suggesting they will sell any product, regardless of any other attributes of quality. Neutral tones offer the greatest security from the ravages of fashion, though their prominence in the league tables of style will still vary. The great benefit of neutrals is their ability to support and complement a wide range of other colours. So, for example, you might have a primary colour palette for your identity supported by a secondary palette of wilder colours to dip into as occasion takes you.

If colour heralds age, it also belongs to location. Different cultures have developed their own native colours. Some colours and palettes of colours are capable of reminding us of certain locations – Indian or Native American, French, British, African, Caribbean, and many more.

A colour looks different depending upon the lighting conditions under which it is viewed. Light from a normal electric bulb tends to be red, whereas light from a fluorescent tube tends to be blue. For this reason, it is recommended that all colours, where possible, should be viewed in a good neutral light such as natural daylight. The colour of daylight also varies enormously according to the climate, time of day and moisture in the atmosphere. The same blue held in the natural light of the Mediterranean appears quite differently when displayed in the natural light of another area or continent.

How a colour is seen also depends on the substance and expanse of the coloured surface being viewed. A large surface area tends to reflect more light, therefore lightening the colour, whilst a smaller surface area tends to darken a colour.

Colours react differently when mixed, mismatched, combined or contrasted with each other. In simple terms, opposite colours improve one another, whilst others struggle to complement each other with varying degrees of success. Many an identity can be immeasurably improved by retuning the colour opposites. Unbalanced colours jar and jangle the senses. For example if your identity is presently red and green, make sure the two colours are exactly opposite on the colour wheel, whatever the brightness or dullness of their hue. Your designer will be able to explain such principles. Basic colour management

– knowledge of the mechanics of colour together with at least some general idea of colour psychology – is a necessary skill for all those involved in identity design and management. All you need to know is that the message of colour travels at the speed of light. What you say, or how pleasing something is to touch, taste or smell, arguably lags behind this first sensation. For most this is automatic, undeniable and unavoidable. Blind people escape this confusion, exploring their other senses first – in fact they are less confused by other senses. Whatever your sense preference, justify the colours you use and be in control of this major component of your identity.

Often the choices people make are by persuasion of colour alone. Sometimes a manufacturer may either guide or restrict the colour choice available, with good intention. A range of products may be suited best to a small range of colours or colour combinations. Restricting the available choice controls the taste of the identity – and the identity of product in the field. Imagine perhaps advertising your identity twenty-five years from now. It might be important.

The use of colour is not necessarily good for your health. Certainly not all colours suit you – either on a personal dress level or as an organisation. The influence of colour cannot be underestimated. Our personal likes and dislikes form a map in our minds of what appeals and that which we would rather avoid. Some people as well as markets are more colour sensitive than others. Some of your staff's skin colour suits that snazzy new blue and red uniform you are about to introduce, but it will not suit everyone's complexion. Conscious of our colour preferences or not, we all make, or are subjected to, a daily bombardment of colour choices at home, work or play, as our home decor, office, cars and clothing all testify.

some people are more colour sensitive than others

Some colours calm whilst others excite: for example, a red interior for a passenger aircraft would seem less suitable than a calm blue. In a sports car, the excitement of red may be desirable. As a gentleman, a pink evening suit may be the most desirable item in your wardrobe or the most unlikely. What is true is that some colours (and, it should be said, textures, shapes and patterns) produce sharp differences in opinion, whilst the appeal or acceptance of others remains less controversial. Certain colours may be acceptable amongst only a narrow range of the particular audience you are addressing, for taste in colour is so often a signal of membership. Signal your acceptance of the status quo or renounce it by controversial use of colour; whether the choice is unwitting or deliberate, the effect is likely to be the same. Colour can equate to snobbery and division.

Colours are often associated with a certain product or production method. Such products often enjoy a history, originating from a region or other cultural area, such as the local soil colour or byproduct of a mining process. The associations of these customary colours may be deep-rooted. If you choose to turn your back on custom or heritage, do so by adopting a profitable shock or advantage.

Pink might denote homosexual to one, or a reggae music label to another. British Racing Green might denote the heydays of 1950s British motor racing to you, Robin Hood, or the 'timeless' décor of the gentleman's club down the road. Threads of time associations are there to be exploited. If your name is 'Green', then your corporate colour scheme almost certainly has a need to be green, unless the avoidance of such an obvious colour choice can be seen to be both a deliberate and profitable disruption of expectation. Furthermore, if you choose to use green (or any other colour) ensure the pigment matches the perceived age of the identity you wish to project. All colours have a history of availability and development. In other words, different pigments represent different periods of technology and chronology.

Select your colour schemes through a process of thought and elimination. The truth is that of the thousands of colour shades available most can be dismissed for one reason or another. Firstly, many will be unsuited to your industry or marketplace. Others will need to be avoided for reasons of competition. All will need justifying in relation to your firmwords, combined with an acute understanding of your products or services.

For example, in Test 6 on page 102 some firmword combinations were shown. Taking just one combination of firmwords from the examples shown might produce the following train of discussion:

Geometry – Art : Active

These firmwords have been selected for a leading producer of computer-aided design software. Their products are the most advanced available, providing a virtual reality display, with integrity, from the data programmed by the engineer or other creative operator. This data also produces detailed drawings and a raft of other essential information, including all component lists.

Active – certain colours in nature belong to activity, others to more static phenomena. The word 'active' demands colours bright or light enough to suggest the possibility of transformation or movement. In which case, chocolate brown would seem less mobile than beige, which would seem markedly less energetic or moving than a bright yellow, vivid blue, bright white or flame red. Certainly the products being promoted are aspiring to the future, rather than the safety of the past. 'Older' colours should be avoided. More forward-looking colours should be employed. Hence the call for active – a movement towards the future.

Geometry – applies to natural law, as we understand it. This may be interpreted as primary colours, colours to signify the underlying dynamics of nature. Alternatively, due to the abstract nature of higher mathematics, bright synthetic colours, indicative of leading-edge enquiry and experimentation, may on occasion fit. But these 'experimental colours' are unproven and, if this firmword relates to a discipline of proven law, would be unsuitable. This distinction would depend upon the nature of the organisation and products being identified and promoted. In this case, the integrity of the computer data is an essential attribute of the product. So any colour misrepresenting the ultimate truth or conclusion of a project, let us say an ambiguous colour, would be unsuitable.

Art – encompasses all the colours of a painter's palette. We would need to establish the nature of the painter's style. The other firmwords in this combination – geometry and active – suggest modern art rather than any other period or style. When one thinks of art and geometry, the artist Mondrian springs to mind. Again, bright and bold primary colours would suggest a confirmation of the suggested colours of geometry.

The nature of this exploration needs to be experienced within the realms of a real situation – organisation and product – so that the finer points of the argument can be seen in an accurate light. By this method suitable colours can be identified and experimented with in terms of proposed logo designs, typefaces, sample literature or other visuals. Even so, a degree of abstract reflection is required – a common process for professional designers to partake in, but not necessarily enjoyed by all. What should be clear is that there exists a framework for directing and containing worthwhile discussion and exploration about the values of some colours in preference to others. Without this desire to justify colour usage, you operate by your personal instincts, or the instincts of others, alone. Even if these instincts are enlightened, can you convey or share them consistently and rapidly with others who may also need to work on the project with you?

In this way, the use of colour and the decision-making process employed to justify it should be managed, rather than left alone, as they so commonly are.

GENDER GAMES

It is worthwhile asking yourself how masculine or feminine your identity appears to be through its presentation and content. The answer will depend on the character of the organisation or product being promoted as well as audience preference. Notions of sexual orientation, including the option of sexual neutrality, are both noticeable and manageable through visible features such as shape and colour as well as attitudes and mannerisms. For example, depending upon the audience politics of taste and attitude, the application of certain colours will be suggestive of gender, however pronounced or subliminal these suggestions may be. Likewise, the weight and shape of typefaces and other decorative graphical elements hold potential connotations of sexuality.

When these factors are combined, whether consciously or unconsciously, they become most persuasive. These together with all other signals affect the five senses, including smell, which, although perhaps the least likely of them all to influence an identity, is important for some organisations, such as those in the cosmetics industry and an increasing number of others, including retailers and the service industry. Smell is a valuable and undeniable component, and like good lighting can create ambience and atmosphere. Like muzak in a retail area, smell is not necessarily consciously noticed. When it is, we tend to form an opinion, or an unconscious recognition becomes evident. Why else do we become compelled to categorise the scent of perfumes into notions of his or hers, or else consciously promote them as being cross-sexual? In so many other ways, smell categorises our experiences, such as the smell of a hospital, or even entire industries.

Pour femme or homme colour too, such as the issue of pink or powder blue or the neutral alternative of primrose yellow for the newborn baby's nursery (or the deliberate avoidance of all three), will exercise the minds of many a parental home decorator. But it also exerts a wider influence, such as the choice of décor for a passenger terminal, the exterior and interior colour schemes for a range of automobiles, the predominant colour on a brochure or uniform. Be aware that there will be many crucial or sensitive colour decisions where merely choosing the wrong colour may wreak havoc upon the desired identity simply because of a contradiction or confusion you have unwittingly presented to your audience. In addition, even if you do not share the superstitions or traditions of your audience, you should make sure that you are aware of the gender boundaries you may be crossing.

Deliberate gender-crossing, for example a logotype or other graphic with a heavy typeface of masculine appearance – such as an ultra bold or Egyptian slab serif font – for a predominantly female product, where a degree of finery or sensitivity would normally have been expected, can be effective if you can be certain of controlling the controversy that cross-dressing can cause. Through stark contrast, in this example presented in a defiance of common custom or expectations, you may have created a powerful and overt statement of daring. Alternatively, you may be disastrously off the mark. The subject matter often dictates beyond negotiation this balance of gender, but then again it is often through breaking conventions that we can create the most startling differential. Convention-breaking is at least a temporary attention grabber, if nothing else.

On first analysis, an earth-moving machine hardly seems to be a feminine product. But imagine that this particular contractor is owned and operated by female personnel within a nation or culture where this would still be considered to be unusual. If so, the marketing department may realise that this disruption of expectations (and the controversy it therefore produces) provides useful publicity and is therefore a positive addition to the identity launch.

In summary, considerations of gender can be finely argued down to the smallest of details. Often an identity must exist as a mixture of differing gender signals in order to reflect both its staff and audience's preferences alike. Even so, some areas of an organisation's business can benefit or suffer through deliberate or indiscreet application. This is regardless of any notions or legislation relating to sexual equality.

Consistency

IDENTIFIABLE MASS

The binding element of identity is consistency, for consistency creates conformity, and if there is no conformity there can be no identifiable mass.

You need to ask yourself whether your identity belongs to you, your direct competition or the identifiable mass of your perceived market area. It is easy to lose definition of identity in this manner. Your identity needs critical mass. An audience needs to be able to clearly recognise your sameness, but not necessarily because this sameness is a consistency also shared by your competitors, for that is merely conformity with others. You certainly require conformity with yourself; a trueness of self; a consistency of self. Where this conformity also spills into representing conformity with the competition is another matter for you to decide upon.

Consistency creates predictable, which in turn creates trust. Consistency creates something far more powerful than most realise: it creates the valuable asset of predictability. The presence of predictability is vital if you are to create trust, and in return trust creates an outcome that both you and the audience can mutually benefit from.

consistency creates predictable, creates trust

Of course what we trust can be consistently either good or bad. You can be trusted to be consistently either. The important point is that trust is the fabulous by-product of consistency. If your identity lacks predictability it must therefore be inconsistent. If you are inconsistent you succeed in communicating potential confusion and therefore the possibility of distrust. Depending on the sophistication of your audience, you may be confusing them.

149

Consistency by itself does not guarantee that your audience will have a favourable opinion of you but, as a result of what they believe to be your consistency, they will have identified you. This can be excellent if it results from planning, but ultimately unhealthy if by default. Beware that although the unplanned can produce accidental success, it can just as accidentally be destroyed.

Consistency is the invisible force that underlies an identity. Yet surprisingly it is frequently abused and mismanaged by those who fail to understand its true meaning or value. Often the owner of a successful identity will damage that same success through a lack of understanding: they fail to comprehend the nature and importance of their consistency and therefore allow it to fracture, weaken or break irreparably. Just like a reputation, consistency can always stand improvement, but it is much harder to repair once damaged, and easily broken beyond repair.

Do not be surprised to find that the realisation of consistency plays such a crucial role in all our day-to-day decision-making. We consciously or unconsciously seek confirmation through the recognition of patterns. There is a need to recognise patterns. With patterns we can more confidently predict. The more pronounced the patterns we notice, whether or not we fully understand their importance to us, the more secure we will feel about the decisions being made. It just might be your sixth sense, because whether you believe in the existence of a sixth sense or not you are nonetheless forced to use your skills of prediction whenever you must decide between products, services, organisations or individuals. You may be deciding on a new car; a charity to make a donation to; a gas station to refill your fuel tank; an airline to fly with; a job offer to a prospective employee; a new career move; a church to attend; a marriage partner – you name it.

consistency is the invisible force that underlies an identity

Your criteria for these decisions are based on the performance you seek versus the pattern of performance you detect. Your brain is a pattern detector! Detection includes the recommendations of others, publicity and advertising campaigns (including those you thought you couldn't remember) and your direct experience (regardless of limitations) with the subject you are compelled to judge. You scan for information to satisfy your desired level of trust and preference for predictability. The core of this examination is based upon your demand for consistency.

The underlying strength of your identity depends on this consistency. Long or short term, your audience will gauge you on this pattern and performance. Your values may not be the same as theirs – indeed, they may neither recognise nor agree with your values – or not yet. Perhaps you may even hope as much. Maybe by the time others finally recognise your objectives you may have already long left the market; or perhaps emerged as the leader you always knew you were...

Think about this in terms of your own decision-making. To what extent do you find a purchasing decision hard work? The answer may depend upon the subject matter, for this may determine your interest. Some subjects hypnotise more than others. Perhaps you shy away from detail or perhaps you revel in it. Either way, notice how you automatically become engaged in forming a decision based upon the recognition of a pattern that suits your need, and patience.

It takes concentration to remain still long enough for others to identify your position, or for you to study theirs. Perhaps, like me, your ability to concentrate is often selective, fickle, sometimes inattentive or just plain lazy.

we all tend to think that inconsistencies reveal the truth about a product or an organisation

The first pattern to be perceived and accepted (the first impression) may prove conclusive for some; subsequent patterns which become revealed later either confirm the first pattern or contradict. Confirmation of consistency breeds trust, contradiction breeds confusion.

Ask yourself what opinion you form of individuals who seem to contradict themselves by inconsistent behaviour, dress or appearance? Whatever the identity being viewed, recognising a pattern depends upon spotting the pattern repeat. No repeat and the design appears to be random.

In other words, it remains unknown or unpredictable because there is no element that we can be certain will be repeated. We may find ourselves making consistency judgements on the slimmest of evidence. Perhaps the item, individual or organisation is new to you. You simply do not have enough information to make any accurate appraisal of their consistency. Yet the urgency to do so may be impossible to resist. Regardless of any firm information available, if the identity on view is offering the right manner and level of visual consistency, you will most likely be satisfied. The product proposition of the identity might be very attractive in all other respects, but a lack of appropriate consistency can still mean market failure. Your audience may ultimately feel too insecure to purchase, even if your product is better and your price better value. A common solution can be redressing it with a more appropriate level of consistency.

It is the failure to recognise a pattern that promotes insecurity, whilst recognition is comforting. You might also like to reflect on how clothed in secrecy you or your organisation appears to those inside or outside. Even if the world reads your advertisements, does your identity remain a barrier to greater understanding? Is your consistency unmistakable? Do your players know what team they are playing in? Does the centre forward know who the left back is? And anyway, where's the football? Why are you passing me a baseball? And he thinks it's cricket.

The sophistication of the pattern determines the ease with which it is identified. This defines the target audience: the easier the pattern, the larger the catchment area. Likewise, the more sophisticated the pattern, the more it may act as a barrier – admitting only a more select audience – or, if coded sufficiently, an otherwise secret organisation.

Ask yourself how many organisations you encounter which alienate you with either too much sophistication or too little. Sophistication of pattern is no pattern if the audience is unable to see it. Too easy, too hard, the visual patterns you construct in the minds of the audience operate the barriers and doorways to the content your identity may promise. To a major extent this determines your accessibility and eventual audience, depending on that audience's desire or definition of sophistication. One audience, or section of an audience, may find a simple pattern offputting, perhaps even crude. Another audience may find a simplistic pattern, especially a deliberately simplified one, not just easily understandable, but perhaps even suggestive of an equality they positively wish to associate themselves with – and be seen to associate with. In such ways the pattern complexity of an identity versus the sensibilities of the audience have a lot to do with inclusion or exclusion.

A pattern too dense or complex may threaten if perceived as a social code by a section of the audience who may as a result feel unconfident or unable to understand the subtleties of the presentation before them. Through fear or prejudice they may retreat before you. Perhaps this is a useful idea. If not, think again, for like the language and complexity of the vocabulary you use to speak with, you must also carefully consider the signals you send towards the eyes of those who see you.

sophistication of pattern is no pattern if the audience is unable to see it

Test 8 · sophistication of pattern

This test is the comparison of two illustrated patterns:

▎ Pattern 1 – a simple pattern that creates a simple certainty. It is easily understood with only a small area visible.

▎ Pattern 2 – a more complex pattern which may pass undetected. The work involved in discovering the pattern may frustrate you. Or, it may flatter your ego because you have the ability or knowledge to identify whilst others fail.

1

2

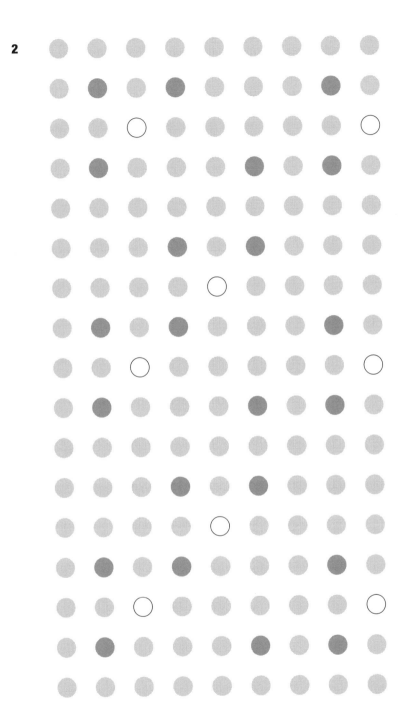

Test 9 · pattern failure

▌ Pattern 3 – a perceived error within a pattern becomes a focus of attention.
The pattern becomes questionable or disappears altogether. Once spotted,
such mistakes can become more recognised than the otherwise intended pattern.

Though it is possible that what you see represents part of a much larger whole,
with the information on offer you cannot be certain.

Notice how a focal point is a powerful way to demand attention – whether deliberate or not. A focal point is difference. Having set in motion a canvas of consistency, any abnormality, planned or otherwise, will promote itself. Through contrast it will stand out clearly. It will demand attention.

This is a double-edged sword: the error gets punished all the more, whilst the planned appearance of a deliberate highlight gains powerful prominence.

any abnormality, planned or otherwise, will promote itself

Unfortunately, and all too commonly, it is the highlighted mistake which gains the most attention. All too often this is self-inflicted. These mistakes commonly occur just because the consistency necessary for the identity to operate successfully is not sufficiently understood or acknowledged.

For many the issue of consistency is akin to boredom. 'Always the same' proves frustrating for those who tire of repetition – which will on occasion may include most of us, especially when we lose the thread of the reasons and objectives of the identity. There is a need to beware of action or change prompted simply by restlessness or tedium. Remain alert to the waning concentration of the marketing department bored through an unfocused desire for stimulation, when the real stimulus should be the ultimate goal of the overall identity.

3

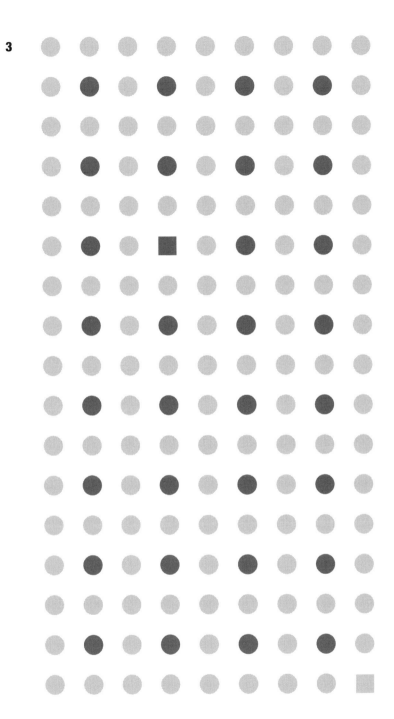

<blockquote>
Pattern 4 – as is evident from Pattern 3, those who underestimate the importance of consistency when displaying their logo, or other elements of their identity, deliver these errors directly to their target audience.

Imagine 'Logo 1' is the logo of a company as displayed throughout its premises, advertising and literature.
</blockquote>

At first glance, the logo may appear generally consistent. It certainly reads the same. Yet only five of these logos are strictly identical. Some inconsistencies are more obvious than others. You should take time to note your degree of blindness to these.

Be careful, because what you currently see as an acceptable level of consistency may not be consistency at all.

INCONSISTENCIES

Once inconsistencies become apparent to an audience, they will inevitably be seen to represent a lack of systematic management or procedure. They must decide whether this inconsistency is deliberate or accidental. If the logo is inconsistent, then why should the integrity of that company's products prove to be any different? And, though you have not yet been introduced to them, what expectations do you have about this company's sales force? 'Erratic' is a word that springs to mind.

All this through the sole presentation of the logo, the tip of a much greater whole identity. Beyond the presentation of the logo itself patterns of consistency should be implemented at all levels of your communication, however insignificant some may at first appear. Your zeal for achieving not only consistency of appearance, but ever-increasing standards of the same in all your identity says and does will repay you in producing an identity of immense improvement and strength. Strong because all muscles pull in the same direction. Consistent because you do what you say you will do. You appear predictably predictable as a matter of standard expectation. Your consistency appears remarkable because competitors with less determination cannot match your continuity or regularity.

4   **Logo 1**   **Logo1**   **Logo 1**

LoGo 1   **logo1**   **LOGO 1**

Logo 1   Logo 1   Logo 1

Logo 1   **L o g o 1**   **Logo 1**

LOGO 1   LOGO•1   Logo 1

Logo 1   **Logo 1**   **Logo 1**

Logo 1   **Logo 1**   **Logo 1**

You can take this to whatever extremes you desire. Let us consider just the regular size and positioning of a logo.

> ▮ Pattern 5 – unlike Pattern 4, these logos are consistent and therefore present a united appearance. Notice now how the whole becomes greater than the sum of parts – that consistency compounds.
>
> Comparing Pattern 4 with Pattern 5, which company (Logo 1 or Logo 2) gives you the greatest confidence?

You may also ask yourself which of the two promises to keep its word. Now realise how much can be achieved through such an easy application of effort. What the organisation of Logo 2 offers in services or other content has not been discussed. We do not know what they do or how well they do it. Yet we can easily differentiate between this organisation's logo and Logo 1 as displayed in Pattern 4. There is a difference only quantifiable because of a thin veil of consistency which, despite no other information being available, speaks volumes. In such ways consistency leads an audience's opinions and expectations.

To summarise: to be consistent is to be predictable is to be trusted. It is to become measurable. Another word is 'quantifiable'.

To ram the point home again: your tenacity to be consistent sets the strength of your identity. The greater your perception of consistency and your desire to be consistent, the more strength your identity accrues. If you only pay this issue lip service, you will accordingly limit the strength of your identity. And it is a certainty that whatever level of consistency you have already achieved, there is a higher level to which you should aspire.

However high the actual quality of your product or service is, the consistency of your presentation controls how others may be willing to perceive you. A competitor with lower-grade products or services, who achieves a significantly higher standard of consistency, creates an advantage over you.

So here is your excuse to be a perfectionist and dictate your will throughout your organisation. Become obsessed – it's OK. To some, consistency may be seen as an uninteresting issue of little value – it may even seem counter to the instincts of many – but lack of it is corrosive to your identity.

5   **Logo 2**   **Logo 2**   **Logo 2**

Logo 2   **Logo 2**   **Logo 2**

Logo 2   **Logo 2**   **Logo 2**

Logo 2   **Logo 2**   **Logo 2**

Sadly, most people fail to understand the meaning of consistency. Even if you are nodding your head in agreement with what I have said so far, the chances are you still do not appreciate the commitment required or the degree of visual consistency necessary if your identity is to truly appear regular, disciplined and coordinated. Imagine you have a company which already enjoys some success and that your logo is cherished and much used. You believe it is used consistently, but look again. Take measurements, gather samples, cut them out, copy, stick them on a wall – look. Is what you see before you exactly the same? The same colour, spacing and proportion? Is the logo used consistently, are the supporting elements consistent, is it consistent in size and positioning? The levels of consistency go on. How seriously you challenge yourself and your organisation dictates the potency of your identity. This same potency can prove particularly invaluable when navigating through dramatic periods of change. Consistency pretends continuity and stability, whatever the changes it may be managing to conceal.

To ignore consistency and be consistently inconsistent labels you as an amateur, unless the pattern of chaos is both relevant to the values of your product and its audience, and this inconsistency is (at a higher level) nothing of the sort. Very rarely can anyone behave like this and keep their integrity intact.

The exception might be a performing artist or magician whose very act relies upon creating surprise and therefore unpredictability. Doing this consistently may be crucial to their identity, and skilful management may ensure it becomes integral to their success. However, your inconsistency may be less tolerated.

There are three types of consistency to concentrate on. As stated at the beginning of this chapter, you must ask yourself whether the mass of your identity belongs to you, your direct competition or perceived market area.

CONSISTENCY WITHIN MARKET AREA

Market areas vary between old and established; young and rebellious; new and striving towards becoming established; or categories yet to be invented. In which market area do you choose to reside? You must decide this position.

You must also choose your level of conformity with that market and the competition within it. Is it comforting to your intended audience to be readily identifiable as belonging to a specific sector? If so, what is the identity of this sector? How far should you blend into or stand out from it? Decide your position – and your conformity with the positioning of others – before chance takes over.

If your market area has yet to be defined, who is defining it? Is it the media, your competitors, certain key personalities, or you? Set this market area firmly in mind. Invent your own if needs must. To a large extent all market areas are fictitious areas of common agreement. They exist because people agree on their existence. Fit your identity within the boundaries you choose. Be deliberate.

CONSISTENCY WITHIN AN ORGANISATION

This is the level of consistency within your organisation as understood and communicated by your marketing literature, exhibitions, press releases, signage, shop interior, vehicle livery, uniform and all other communication and display items. In fact, and of course, in everything you do. It is how you manage and regulate everyone within the team – and how you succeed or fail in the process.

In retailing it is irrelevant whether your shop is part of a larger retail chain or a unique outlet with a character of its own. The exterior and interior, stock, presentation and staff should form the shop's own consistency – however individualistic. Your consistency should be deep enough to sincerely match the qualities and values the identity intends to communicate. If not, you appear a fake.

INDIVIDUALITY

An army intending to be seen and identified as a working unit needs to be dressed in the same uniform. If nothing else, it helps to know who to avoid shooting at. Unless you don't care: there is no known uniform for a bandit. A covert force may avoid any form of dress code. Not seeking any visual identity, it literally wants to blend with the market.

But assuming you are a normal member of society, your dress or uniform, as everything else, should be relevant to the identity you wish to project. You have a need to be recognised today as well as tomorrow, next week or next year. A salesperson usually doesn't wear jeans one day, a suit the next, a miniskirt or shorts and a pair of flip-flops every alternate Wednesday and Friday, because confusion of this sort is not useful to his or her recognition or identity. Nevertheless, extremes of inconsistency eventually become consistency: you change uniform every single day because you are an unpredictable creative volcano – or clown – and that is just what you want your audience to believe.

The quest for consistency should never dominate an individual to the point where all individuality ceases, unless your aim is the forced regime of the combat unit or prison camp. In these circumstances the reasons may seem clear and justifiable for the objectives being set. However, the natural law is that people have a need to retain their individuality. This need should be taken into account or else you will surely offend them.

Inside the organisation, for example, you may want all your staff to wear the same red-coloured paper hats in every restaurant you own. You may have decided that it will form an effective part of your new identity, but how will your staff react? It may depend on how much they believe you are removing their individuality, and the validity or commonly shared benefits of doing so.

The suppression of individuality in the interests of greater internal consistency must be treated with diplomacy and care, morale being such a delicate issue of trust and belief. From where else can staff gain their trust but recognition of and agreement with the consistency and values of their leaders?

If you are identified as a member of a group, you assume the values or perceived values of that group. If you judge those values to be worthy, you may be more willing to blend your identity with the greater whole. Otherwise, you resist. Witness children arriving at school in the morning and the differing manner in which they comply with a compulsory dress code. Their attitudes vary from total compliance to partial, individual interpretation or even refusal. Is this refusal the fault of the individual or the school?

Outside, beyond the confines of the organisation, you should not offend the individualism of your suppliers or customers either. Be aware of these boundaries and the actions you take when crossing them. In other words, don't take liberties with the identity of others unless you are prepared to pay the price. There are often situations in business when one identity must become a temporary partner or custodian of another. Often identities have need to support or endorse another. If your organisation is in communications or broadcasting you may well need to present the identities of others as part of your news bulletins or services. These identities may in turn need to quote, endorse or promote you. Regardless, the issue of manners and attention to detail is often more important than some assume. If you respect the identities of others they are more likely to return the same consideration.

Personal consistency is not just uniform appearance. It can also be noticed in non-visual signals such as general attentiveness, willingness, manners, speech, writing, time-keeping and other forms of behaviour.

As with all the forms of consistency, the level and endurance people attain create the combining force that binds together the critical mass and pattern we choose. Your consistency positions you within your marketplace. The pattern can set you apart and plays a major role in the amount of trust people are willing to offer you. You determine who will recognise and trust this pattern of consistency by its level of sophistication. Whatever the complexity of the pattern, you can and should determine the standard of this consistency and remain vigilant of any deviation. The stronger the glue of your consistency, the greater the underlying strength of your identity.

Presence

A SENSE OF MYSTERY

Patterns of consistency also determine the sense of mystery others may view you with. This is worthy of close attention because mystery is capable of drawing or repelling an audience. Everyone of 'significance', that is anyone wishing to stand apart from the crowd, requires an appropriate air of mystery – slight, moderate or extreme – to capture the hearts and minds of their audience.

patterns imply how approachable and available you are

This is obvious to the professional storyteller. Once the reader guesses the conclusion of the plot before conclusion is due, their interest slackens: for they already know the answer. It remains true for governments who, although they may be necessarily democratic and therefore suitably transparent in their dealings, must also, in the interests of social cohesion and validity, retain an appropriate air of respect and status. Status partly relies on mystery. The greater the status desired the greater the mystery necessary to support it . For example, beautiful patterns that others may only partly understand may hold an audience in awe, if only because the materials these patterns depend on, and the scale they are used on, are beyond the average means of the audience. Pageantry is one example, but the lush patterns of the stereotypical high status reception area is another. All patterns imply how approachable and available you are. The emotions these consistencies create in the minds of the audience will help determine expectations of price.

THE SHAPE YOU'RE IN

Closely linked to consistency, status and availability is the management of space. Vacant or filled, it is one of the prime considerations for an identity. 'Space' in the context of your identity includes the economy with which you demand your audience's attention, such as the level of white space you are prepared to fund in an advertisement, or the amount of physical space within a retail area not devoted to actual stock. It also includes the deliberate use of silence or inaction in what you tell or do, such as the amount of territory you allow your customers in terms of instruction, control and interaction as opposed to how aggressively you defend or take from them. Space in such terms is as much an inference as an actuality. You offer or restrict space to suit the customer need in terms of such requirements as value, assurance and liberty. Deliberately 'busy' or territorial can equate to good value, in the same way that a layout for a stack 'em high sell 'em cheap company might accentuate a sense of value. Alternatively, too much space in either printed literature or retail area can effect a sense of luxury and corresponding expense. Decisions like these need managing in the light of your target audience and expected margins. In such ways, just the management of space alone acts as a gateway of acceptance and communication, and all this *before* you layer your proposition with content and sales messages.

consider the deliberate use of silence or inaction

Your identity marks the boundaries of an area that is either physically apparent, psychologically, or both. The borders you define will in turn define your market, areas of operation and the intangible values your identity promotes or defends. Shape both presents and hides bulk. It heralds the content it pretends to contain. It also alters the corresponding shapes of the space that must necessarily surround it. So think carefully about the space – the white space or noise – that surrounds or permeates your identity. Begin to realise its hidden messages of definition, boundaries and differential.

If an identity defines a product and its distribution, it must also restrain them from errors in design and communication. It must prevent unsuitable style or content that they might otherwise unintentionally present. Identity is a filtration system to the outside world, and it better be fit for the job, for this means filtering perceptions of gender and size. The frontiers formed may change over time, edging forwards or backwards to suit the climate of fashion, taste and new technology, but yet still remain a clearly labelled territory. Unless you clearly signpost these territories, you are losing your differential.

Test 10

You may remember these shapes from Test 1 on pages 8–9.
Now choose the shape which best describes your organisation.

Only three shapes to choose from, but one will suit the intuitive personality and subject matter of your organisation more accurately than the others. Whatever your choice, reflect on the reasons for your decision. Do not be surprised if the answer eludes you. This may, at first, seem rather obtuse. After all, shape is a major root of emotional confusion. You may instinctively sense that one shape complements or reflects your nature better than another – and it will – but for many this is a difficult concept to acknowledge or articulate.

You might sense that the defence of a square conforms to your sense of security, or a circle your sense of inclusion, or the edges of a triangle your sense of action. You might also sense a good many other connotations and potential values. The point is that these simplistic shapes are (in turn) shaping your emotional reactions. Within their confusion lies a sense of truth.

Mystery is often a form of beautiful. True beauty defies description. So often judged on shape alone, beauty confounds. It is this unresolved interplay upon the senses, rather than any other precise or understood specification, which fills the eye of the beholder.

Shape, especially when combined with colour, can offer the promise or suggestion of many other attributes such as gender, age, maturity, culture, fitness, vocation, function, subject, wealth, social status and much more.

'How' this is achieved or explained is the domain of the creative and visual literate. 'Why' is a responsibility, which can be shared by all. Trying to explain the near unexplainable can be highly amusing for some. Try asking your designer. It's part of their job description.

Space can indicate the size of the parent organisation, an issue significant to most audiences. An identity dependent on projecting a physical size in order to gain market acceptance should offer a suitable impression of scale. So do not take this lightly. A blank page or an advertisement display area is a shape that will almost always hold a certain significance. The gaps or interaction of the spaces between shapes set the tone of pattern or chaos, as well as the apparent tension, movement or stability of the identity. Some ratios of size and space are more suited to your identity than others. For example, if the size of your hotel accommodation is a defining sales point, you would be unwise to use crammed advertisement space.

It is worth considering that everything has an optimum size and position. Even your number of personnel. Optimum size is performance. Your sense of order another. Every element can and should be positioned correctly. Correct position is instinctively understood once it is seen. Arriving at an understanding of what makes the position of the elements in an identity correct defines the talent of the architect. The point is that some artists are better than others. Just as some colours or shapes can justifiably suit an identity, size and position can work wonders in perception-building. The rules for defining perfect size and position for the elements of your identity should, though, begin with your logo (of whatever variant). Flowing from the logo, these proportions should be an essential part of your final identity guidance.

Illustration 17

Without exception all shapes create the illusion of secondary shapes. For example, these black shapes inevitably create their counterparts: white shapes. Meaningful or meaningless, they are either opportunities or distractions.

Often the perception of another's size rules people, perhaps to the point where they dare not challenge. This is because size is so often indicative of power. Yet what is presented may bend the truth. Clever identity can minimise or exaggerate size at will. Therefore the perceived size you need to project into the market needs to be become an issue of policy. For example, there is also occasion when the best policy is to spell it out loud: tell them you designed 18 of the 26 Chinese power design institutes, and make no bones about it. There will be other situations where small is beautiful, and the pretence of niche is exactly what you should be attempting to preserve, and market domination a truth you would be better off disguising.

Illustration 18

As your organisation grows in stature you will from time to time need to re-evaluate your status. Affirmations of operational size and breadth may need to be represented to your target audience. Here is a graphic that tells more than it is actually telling. In other words, graphic treatment together with tightly edited phrases suggests more than meets the eye.

THE BIGGEST OPEN-FACED COPPER MINE ON THE PLANET

MORE THAN 50% OF UK NORTH SEA OIL PRODUCED IS BY ROWDEN-DESIGNED PLATFORMS

27 OF THE WORLD'S LARGEST 30 QUOTED CHEMICAL COMPANIES

THE WORLD'S BIGGEST PERMANENTLY-MOORED FLOATING PRODUCTION PLATFORM 18 OF THE 26 CHINESE POWER DESIGN INSTITUTES

30 MILLION TONNES OF SHIPS PER YEAR AND A MASSIVE 7 OF THE TOP 10 SHIPBUILDERS INCLUDING THE TOP 3

A PLANT THAT PRODUCES ENOUGH TEXTILE TO CARPET AN AREA THE SIZE OF SWITZERLAND EVERY 36 MONTHS

A FLOATING PRODUCTION FACILITY BIGGER THAN LONDON'S CANARY WHARF

A HISTORY OF INNOVATION THAT DOMINATES TODAY'S ENGINEERING IT TERMINOLOGY AND PRODUCTION METHODS

Illustration 19

not necessarily small

Both size and inference of weight can suggest size.

Any audience may pass judgement on size before knowing any or all of the facts. They may believe without further challenge, to suit your aims or hinder them. Many stand fixated by the spell of an identity, both those who own it and those confronted by it, into a state of dumb servitude. Apparent size, whether real or fantastical, has a lot to do with confidence of presentation – the confidence to rule and challenge.

The size of an organisation can be shown without being told. Show is often more powerful than tell. Big is not necessarily greater than small. Size of identity, in this context, means its cumulative effect in the minds of your audience. This might depend upon twenty-four-hour, seven-day-a-week advertising or no promotion at all. It might be commonly available for all to see and understand, or else work quietly but diligently behind the scenes. The size of your marketplace may be immense or diminutive, but size of identity can operate independently of any physical reality. It does so by occupying, or better still, being invited into, the hearts and mind of your audience. You can be a magnified minnow, or a stealth whale. Size is relative. Big or small, it is the grace with which you are seen to manage your space that creates the overall effect of size.

Illustration 20

A sense of order: imagine that this different-sized logo is seen to appear on a variety of badged products and marketing material. This imaginary logo appears exactly to the same specification, but the sizes are erratic.

Logo   Logo   Logo

Logo   Logo   Logo

Logo   Logo   Logo

Logo   Logo   Logo

Logo   Logo   Logo

Logo   Logo   Logo

Logo   Logo   Logo

Illustration 21

A sense of order: compared with the previous illustration, here is the same logo again, but with a system of regulated sizes.

Again, imagine that these different sizes are taken from a variety of badged products and marketing material. Notice the different perception of size and character between the two illustrations.

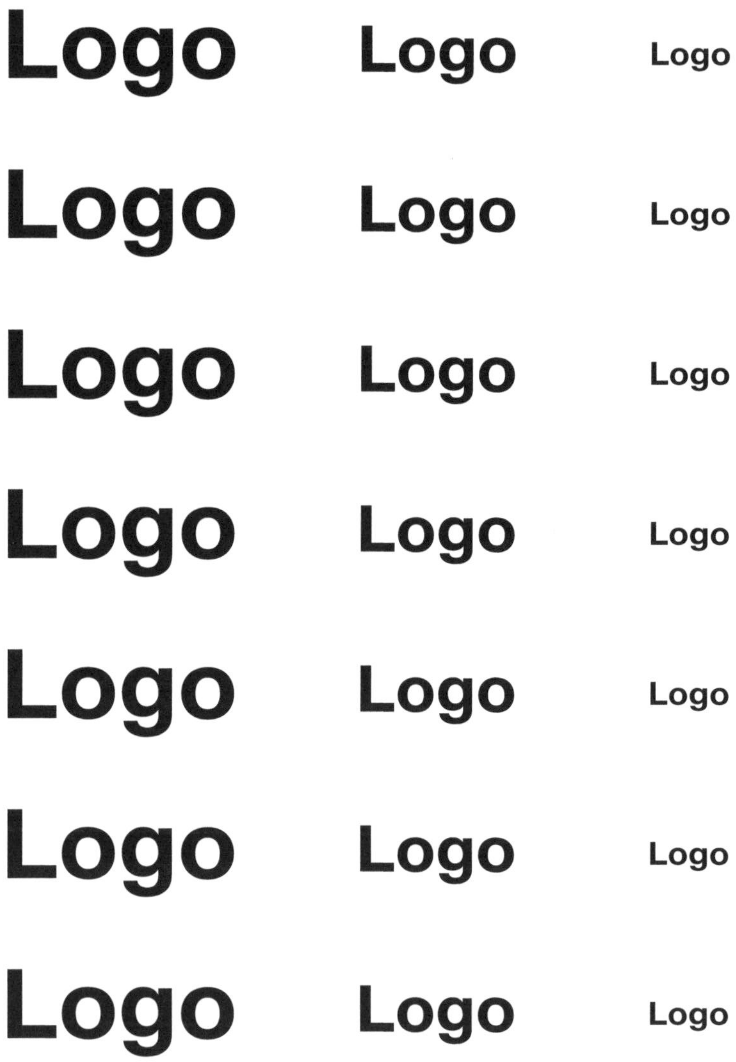

Logo	Logo	Logo
Logo	Logo	Logo
Logo	Logo	Logo
Logo	Logo	Logo
Logo	Logo	Logo
Logo	Logo	Logo
Logo	Logo	Logo

172

SIZE OF ACCESS

For access read availability. How large are your entrances and other interfaces with your audiences outside the organisation? How obvious to find, restrictive and navigable are they? Obviously this includes physical entrances, such as to buildings, but more importantly all interfaces, such as literature and websites. Even the size of your logo infers a sense of availability. How hard does it try to gain your audience's attention? How large often equates with how vulgar. A pinch smaller might take you up market, a pinch larger might make you appear more populist. Such signals and consistencies of size, however insignificant they might first appear to you, do indicate a sense of restriction and availability.

The regulation of space and size of access is, where practical, the restriction of the key elements of your identity to a series of fixed sizes. For example, limiting the size of a logo to few fixed-sized appearances regulates appearance. Although the management of this is likely to remain undetected by the audience, it creates a significantly higher level of consistency beyond the norm. It brings in a sense of order, and if order is a necessary audience value, you would be foolish not to do this.

Identity manages the choreography – appearance as well as frequency of appearances. It is important to employ conditions of size and space wherever possible. In particular, use space as a ratio of understandable increments. This is where sophistication and consistency of pattern, as described in the previous chapter, lend clarity and power. Just such simple management of size and disciplined order determines the overall strength and nature of an identity.

a pinch smaller might take you up market

In more general terms, the use of size and the frequency of visibility with which an identity presents itself in a marketplace helps create the impression that others have about the willingness or wish of the organisation or product to be available. Consider whether the identity in question appears on every street corner, lives in a big house on the hill or is hidden in the back streets.

Illustration 22

Three entrance signs. A speaks louder than B speaks louder than C.

Illustration 23

Another three signs, again all offering the same invitation, or do they? Consider the inflection of how much they appear to be both offering on the one hand and denying on the other.

Is the product which the identity promotes commonly available? Does the commercial availability of the typeface supporting the logo match this value? Irregular or restricted availability or access might result in only limited publicity or recognition. The smaller organisation may lament this apparent limitation of promotion as the reason for any lack of success. Yet limited promotion or the uncommon can also mean exclusivity: if the identity, product and marketing affirm this in unison, and if the self-confidence of the identity is both well founded and strong enough to refuse, or appear to refuse, business it does not desire. In other words, an identity is discerning, and shares this discrimination with its intended audience, those initiated, who in turn may also willingly allow a corresponding increase in your profit margins.

Like a drawbridge you defend or open your sense of security and accessibility. Even the intercharacter spacing on a line of type, especially within your logo, will signal your focus. Each character should almost, but not quite, touch and the space between each word should be no more than a lower-case 'i'. Study your nearest high street and notice what businesses do just that, and how differently you judge them to those businesses that do not. Alternatively, if you are promoting Georgian-style conservatories, you should take note of period typefaces that were originally designed for the wider character spaces of the then printing technology. Tight spacing is modern, big business and organised. Sloppy spacing is small business, amateur and provincial.

Appearing too available can be as counter-productive as being unavailable: both can drive you out of business. What your intended audience may prefer in relation to what is best for your objectives is a matter for you to decide. You may have only one doorway to the street or, for that matter, the world, but if it is well considered, it may be the only entrance required. If you are offering a wide choice of entrances (telecommunicative or physical), ensure they suit your audience's needs: synchronised order or deliberate diversity.

DEFEND YOUR OWN SPACE

Consider how welcoming, purposeful or confusing these points of contact with your audiences are. They cannot be studied often enough. Closely and critically observe the arrival of all those who visit these points – in terms of volume, manner of arrival, ease of navigation and the preferences, pleasure, frustration, embarrassment or awkwardness of those who enter. Fine tune the entrances accordingly. Then do it again later. Make it a habit.

Upmarket or downmarket, your self-management of space reveals how you respect and value the space of others, for if space is a luxury for some, it represents wastage for others.

Then there are issues of defensive space. There is a need to defend an identity from mistreatment by its own organisation and others. All identities have an inner sanctuary that must remain pollution free.

Start with the simple process of determining the defendable space which should surround your logo.

Illustration 24

All logos should have a defensive area into which no other unauthorised graphic element – or edge of display area – may intrude.

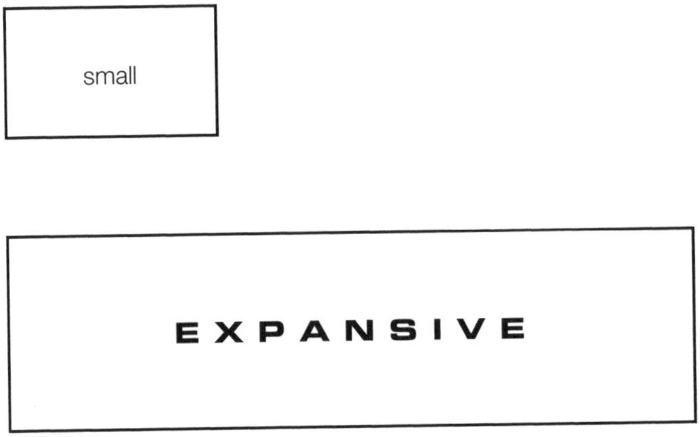

```
┌─────────────────────────┐
│                         │
│         small           │
│                         │
└─────────────────────────┘
```

```
┌───────────────────────────────────────────────────┐
│                                                     │
│              E X P A N S I V E                      │
│                                                     │
└───────────────────────────────────────────────────┘
```

Time

NOTHING STANDS STILL

No smug summing up of differential sticks for long. It is best to view your identity as being an active issue and not something that can be left standing still. Past reputation – the illusion of a fixed point in time – should not be allowed to become a straitjacket for future reputation. To acknowledge instability and enquire into its nature is to remain sensitive. Imagine the market as a big white glacier. It moves slowly, but it can also move suddenly and without warning. Who are those who say they stand still?

Technology and terminology are always moving. Words become redundant or transmute in unhelpful ways to those who were relying on no change. No position, however determined, is a safe haven. We hear so much about change management, but it cannot be emphasised enough that without acceptance of market change an identity is voting to live in the past, and the past is the opposite of the current direction of the market. Don't be fooled by trends for retro design. All design is part retro. History is reinterpretation.

know your time deviations and why

Timing is a major feature for identity as much as it is for a business strategy. This is not just the actual age of the organisation, product or technology but about those signals of apparent age that your identity is radiating. There are obvious measurements, such as the percentage of readers returning an advertising coupon in a magazine; then the less than obvious drivers, such as the headline or image that motivated that response; and then, less tangible again, the emotive associations of layout,

177

typeface and colour. All such design elements have a history of development and usage, so if you elect to use a typeface designed in the 1950s for a presentation alluding to any earlier era, let us say the alternative glamour of the 1920s, then know your time deviations and why. Even the use of 'white' space carries connotations of period and social grace, if only because it is assumed that the wealthy can afford the luxury of 'wasted' space more than those on tighter budgets, and quantity in terms of printing and media has always been been more affordable to some than others. More obviously there is the lineage of language and its use; material availability and choice, such as wood or plastic laminates; the history and fashion of dress and mannerisms. The list is endless.

Often a combination of timings will need to coexist within your identity. For example, a young organisation for which youthfulness is a positive driver may also 'use' contrasting elements of establishment (for which you need history!) such as antique furniture or old technology, mixing them with leading-edge artefacts and furnishings. But they can only successfully and intelligibly achieve this if they rationalise to their firmwords. In other words, be as eclectic as you wish, regardless of age, providing the common denominators between these objects or characteristics bind all together at that point where identity energises and excels: your firmwords.

BRAND TIME

Consider that we can divide time into the past, present and future. We can apportion everything in this way. We tend to be automatically consumed with this process anyway. Most of us spend a great deal of time thinking about the past, sifting through it, refiling it, editing it. With similar enthusiasm we often conjecture too far into the future, adopting completely impractical stylisations and fashion within our identity's language and presentation, but only because we think this is where it is all going. In short, we estimate impressions of the past or future.

These perceptions of 'past', 'now' and 'future' times become useful containing areas for perception-building. However arbitrary it appears these classifications are, they help order the messages we receive. The relevance of this is when we begin to consciously tune the time perceptions of our audience. This is not complicated and, as a method, it has nothing necessarily to do with the timing of product launch, though it has everything to do with market penetration and longevity. When we speak the name of an identity or brand we also sift through these associations. We may have never purchased the product. It matters not. That we pretend any opinion is what counts. These miscellaneous linkages of memory, whether fact or fiction, hint at the experience we perceive. It is our present reality. Of course, this may not match the intention of the manufacturer's product definition or the experiences and opinions of other consumers. Whether this experience is repeated elsewhere within the manufacturer's target audience is for the identity manager to know. In this complex morass of opinion, half-fact, experience and rumour, the expectations of your audience reside. These are partly drawn from deliberate messages, and elsewhere through the accidental and the sometimes more irrational associations of those who view you.

If your identity or brand focuses only in the past or present or future, see how you limit your market share. It takes an unusual audience to be satisfied with one alone. Credibility demands evidence of progression, not just passing glory or future delivery. Some speculative investors might want to take the risk, but customers might not accept the same vision. The trouble is that proof is only found in the present and past. Future proof is indicating you have a future built on the present. If you do not promise a future at all, or infer it in any part of your overall marketing effort, then address that too. Your shareholders might appreciate some optimism. It is often a tacit communication that there is no particular forward movement or anything else left to fulfil. The oldest of brands continue to develop and mature if given some relevance to the future, however slight. Strategic sponsorship of futurist events or other research charity – an investment in the future – may do wonders for a confectionery product whose identity is otherwise perceptually stuck in the 1930s. Relevant yesterday and tomorrow suggests enduring.

To summarise this, consider that a secure and stable brand spreads its weight across all three time zones. The balance may be, at any given time, or on any given occasion, balanced significantly towards just one, or two of the three, but in total encompassing all three aspects. If you omit or lack sufficient credibility in any one area of these time zones then you increase your vulnerability to the waves of fashion and the gradual failure of growth is yours:

the identity breathes more shallowly; it becomes unhealthy in its unfashionable dying (or denial). In short, remain alert, or present an unbalanced personality: the time-dysfunctional identity.

FASHION

Whether personally fashionable or not, we should remain aware. Anyone charged with the position of identity leadership has a responsibility to ride fashion. The twists and turns of current debates, opinions and tastes are all of potential concern. To miss a minor change in legally, technologically or socially driven change might mean we get things terribly wrong.

Fashion can be likened to a series of waves. They are potentially incoming. Some will be benefit, some will threaten. The issue is unpredictability. Most of us could be forgiven for believing that this is remotely decided elsewhere by those who exert their opinions independently and regardless of ours. Unless we are one of those rare prophets of design, divvying the cosmic pulse of the universe, and confident enough to believe beyond doubt that we are permanently tuned in – a few exist – the successful tracking of fashion is an issue far larger than the average mind can accommodate. For that reason, wave-watching is usually beyond the responsibility of just one person.

given time, most street culture is hijacked

The greater tangibility of recognising what the fashionable have already recognised themselves is far easier. Fast-followers act differently. They pause for others to rally to the first wave then, learning through observation, dive in soon after. For others the thought of following negates the values of their identity. Perhaps they are renowned for being instinctive leaders.

Let's get personal. If you find yourself alone in a crowd, wearing a rubber bathing hat with fluffy pink feathers stuck on top for extra effect, and you are the only one wearing one, then you are either a fashion guru ahead of your time, or a hopelessly off-beam eccentric who stands no chance of ever being so. However, if next week you see others following your lead, then you are possibly on the transitional edge of a new wave. Then you can decide whether it remains a wave you wish to continue riding, or is time to look for the next.

In this way the greater mass of popular code overwhelms the more singular contribution that we alone feel we can offer. If we are bold enough not to care, and stylish enough to forever maintain our balance, then perpetual fashion might just belong to us. For most, the sweeping opinions of others tend to swamp all individuality with barely a whimper. These crushing tides of change may unexpectedly turn on some seemingly invisible, yet pivotal, event of the day. This is either acknowledged in the moment by those with the right antenna or else, several aeons later, in the post-rationalisation of (eventually) a TV documentary or historical book. We all have personal evidence of living through these changes of fortune, yet for the most part might also feel relatively detached from them. After all, we live our days through what are often cited as historic times (aren't they all?) without always feeling the more personal connection with what is later on reported as though it belonged to us all.

The history of products and their identity belongs to that same wider humanity, whilst our more personal experiences, our recognition and participation ultimately and more personally reside only within us. Ah, we might say, so that's why we feel lonely at times. Yes, that is true. If we are honest with ourselves we can all sense our occasional remoteness from one another, and therefore swimming in the shoals of fashion might make us feel less so.

This distinction between the public and the private is a recurring concern for all identities, because the divide is so often clumsily handled. The identity of the audience is often trodden on by the insensitive strategy in a hurry. This concerns much more than just common decency, it is the finer definition of relationship so often ignored by the glut of those vying for our attention. We are all sitting in the audience, and it is our personal experiences of what this feels like that we should be guided by. Most identities might appear to be more interested in their own vanity than their customers. For them, if they were to stop and observe, they might find their version of self-service means more than it might at first more superficially appear, and that the navigation of fashion is something they see as only working one way: as emanating from only their production lines. Leaders and followers become confused: many mistakenly think it is they who power the waves, when all they do is ride. In the case of a service-based product it may be a shallow or false ideal of partnership, or business dressed as friendship, such as the word 'society' within a mortgage company's name. For too many customers the servicing may be only one way.

KNOWING WHAT OTHERS DON'T

The true street savvy knows untruth when they see it. That's why the true fashion revolutionaries refuse the clumsy commercialisations of the fashions that they themselves originally played a part in creating. It is also the reason why they continually recreate and change ahead of the mainstream who, given time, are likely to follow and then swallow their original and regurgitate it as bland. It is not that they won't go along with a producer or retailer who, knowingly or not, serves their needs. Yet once they see the day of the 'counterfeit' fashion approaching – especially counterfeit users wearing 'their' original – the offence of the mismatch has the same effect. They vacate the original and burn the memory with scorn. If by correlation that includes the retailer, producer or brand, the new stigma is distributed accordingly. Whether this derision, the consistency and volume of which will vary, develops into a wider opinion, and for how long this effect will last, will depend. You really do reap the mess you sow – fractured metaphor, but precisely the same crime the product in question might rightly stand accused of.

The same highly fashion-attuned know that, given time, most street culture is hijacked and adapted by what then become the rich-kid brands of mass acceptance. This broadening of what was a more finely focused and privately shared identity is betrayed. Big business aping the fashions of the few is not a trend. It has always been so. Seasoned early adopters remain buoyant and unsubmerged, because they know the precise differences between original and fabricated. In particular, our children are by no means as unaware of these shades of difference as so many adults may, in the forgetfulness of their own youth, believe.

So what can you do to protect yourself from fashion? Not a lot; however, as with any activity, we can always reduce some of the risks. Consider that rising waves have a corresponding downward cycle. Note that the rising usually takes longer to complete its course. The early signs of its swell may go unnoticed, and the volume it builds is dependent on many contributory factors. The one thing you can know is that eventually all waves either crash or peter out. Future change is the problem! We might misinterpret it with alarming frequency, but only because we are chasing it so hard. Now, to arrive there in timely fashion is fashion itself.

Names

CALL ME WHAT YOU LIKE

At the centre of your identity is your name. Self-explanatory or abstract in its communication, it is the pivot around which all other elements must attach themselves. Name assists definition of character, suggesting clues of age, gender, nationality and other attributes of personality.

You offer your audience two items: your presentation generally, however welcome, and your name, however noteworthy. A name signals difference. It is a label definable by attitude; a threshold or entrance to that which it represents; direction; past, current or future position; departure or turning; a label of promise or foreboding depending upon audience point of view, whatever the qualities of its signal.

your name names your value

Something, anything, exists because of its label. It need not physically exist: it can just as easily be rooted in the fantasy or abstract imagination of the mind as any other form of reality.

A name is a label asking for recognition, verification or other refusal. If you recognise the label, you may want to enquire further or refuse more information. You may require a reason or other stimulus in order to inspect closer. Is it of profit to you to do so, and do you trust the proposition of the name's supporting identity? Is there a consistency in the use of names that you can understand and accept as being relevant? A major or minor blip on your radar screen, a name indicates there is more than may immediately meet the eye. It offers definition without necessarily hurrying to explode the underlying nature of the substance it presents or conceals. This label may be the first formal or informal notification of what you are about to encounter, and so is an invitation for judgement, though often in combination with other information, appearance or manner. A name endorses – in haze or pin-sharp focus – by association, deed or other information, however scant or available. The role of graphic design is to positively structure this information, complement its written and verbal use and help build a series of positive perceptual values.

If you have no name, you will need to invent one. There may be urgent pressure to decide, as you cannot trade legally without one. The process of searching for and agreeing upon a name can become either a flippant affair or else the beginning of an agonising period of research and contention. Commonly, a name is adopted hastily, with scant regard to how appropriate it may be, not just during the short term but in the distant future. The implications, which may arise through repetitive usage or the unexpected interpretations and constructions of others, also need to be carefully scrutinised. In addition, the problems of not only agreeing a name, but finding it free from negative associations, legal restrictions of trademark and available for web domain registration make this a trying process for some. Ownership of a name is now an issue of estate management. And the world is your back garden.

do not expect too much from a name alone

However, do not expect too much from a name alone. A name can seldom carry the full weight of meaning, marketing and identity by itself, or at least not unaided for any long duration of time. It is merely the label, which represents the greater whole – the pleasing compère or master of ceremonies whose task is to introduce and appear to manage the show. All aspects of an organisation's operations must work in unison behind the name(s) it employs or chooses to promote, supporting the whole in order to achieve the necessary depth and unison of purpose required so as to remain effective. If you have no sensible choice but to work with an existing name, still ask all the same questions.

If a name is a combination of one or more names, question the seniority between one and another. Are all names equal or some more equal than others? Is the new upstart more valuable than the old master, or vice versa? Check which name is subservient to another. Does one name endorse another?

Are any of the words interchangeable as part of a larger identity, for example a product or place name that changes to suit the occasion? Are there any names, or parts of names, likely to be changed or phased out at any point in the future? In this manner consider the components and other issues within the name.

Many expect to achieve notoriety, uniqueness or originality through invention of name alone. The name you choose may be dynamite – good or bad depending on which side of the explosion you stand. Meanwhile, many an otherwise ideal choice of name is eliminated without enough consideration simply because at this early stage – perhaps as a scribble on a notepad – it appears too nondescript.

The larger the geographical area you intend the name to operate within, the more valuable the name which can successfully cross national or cultural boundaries without the interpretation of language. These boundaries can be from one social group to another, market to market or country to country. Certain words, characters or numbers are more widely acceptable than others. A name which excels itself in one area of operation may be commercial suicide elsewhere. Examine the issues of culture in order to decide how best to penetrate each market to the benefit of the whole operation. Consider the potential value of your name, should your identity one day become a true brand, so that other areas of industry can be trademarked as a form of advance security. For example, has your name the potential to be a valuable future property in other industry sectors, either for yourself or others? If another organisation adopted your name in another sector, would their success compromise the perception of your identity within your market sector?

Further mileage is gained when a name also actively contributes towards your objectives through its literal or suggestive use of language, its genuine power of reputation (self-earned or through association with another's reputation) or authority of endorsement. Combined with graphics, its potential to be memorised in the eyes and ears of your audience will be significantly boosted. This certainly includes censoring within the promoted name any unnecessary legalese or words of dubious or defunct value which add little or nothing to the cause.

The durability of a name needs to match that expected of the identity. It needs to work long term on a slow fuse because, for most, long-lived reputation and appeal are ultimately more beneficial and profitable than just initial infatuation. Of course the ideal is to successfully manage both ends of this scale: be powerfully attractive upon first impression and remain so indefinitely. In this regard the graphical treatment of your name is often far more influential than the spelling of the name itself. Dress the name for short or long term, and be aware of the fuse of impact and fashion.

The tonality with which a name is spoken and the rhythm with which it can be read also sets a certain ambience and expectation. These assumptions are connected with associations in the mind of the viewer derived from their personal experience, taste, culture or any other former information, rumour or suspicion. Connotations of character and quality, together with the uniqueness of a name, pitch it into our awareness. Like driftwood on a beach it stays there until swept further or carried away by successive waves.

The impediments of any given name become more obvious when they are being communicated orally. All names need verbal management because the clarity and phonetics of the names you employ are significant to success. Listen to the manner in which you or your team instinctively answer the telephone. Do the names you use need to be spelt aloud in order to clearly or efficiently communicate or enforce? Perhaps the phonetics give rise to certain irritations when used verbally? How often do you find yourself needing to correct an enquirer, in order to prevent confusion? These are alarm bells you should take serious note of. You may be able to counter some of these problems by a change of pronunciation, punctuation or spelling. If not, you should consider changing the name.

Memory of name can be aided to an astonishing degree by visual appearances. Visual presentation is guaranteed to transform any name, often despite being poorly executed. With skilled typographical treatment or added graphics an otherwise unremarkable name can assume a new persona, no longer solely reliant upon the nature of its sound or basic letterform.

Be aware that familiarity escapes proper interrogation. Regardless of the effectiveness of the name you choose, or must use, its ability to make a first impression will, through repeated usage, wane. The shock of the new gradually erodes for all who must, through familiarity, become less sensitive to or mindful of the qualities of its first impression. As though climbing inside the name, assuming it, consuming it or being unwillingly subjected to it, the weary can no longer judge with impartiality. For those past the issue of acceptance, first impressions of the name become demoted, or diluted to a newer level of confusion – a series of other more fundamental experiences, such as the organisation or product itself.

Illustration 25

X!X? XABE! Welcome

gzüs xwyzz ISSSSS?

Halt! qwwoab snoeyy

Nine signs. All are nonsense except for two – a pleasantry and an urgent instruction. Notice how your recognition and confusion divide, your mind gravitating immediately towards the messages you do understand.

Meanwhile, those who yet remain to be attracted or convinced may, depending upon the nature of their introduction, only notice or begin to do so by the flag-waving of your name alone. Hence the strain to force into the invention of a new name far more import than it is fair to expect it to contain. Reputation needs to be earned. It must follow name – hopefully with the minimum of delay – but the name cannot contain reputation from zero hundred hours, launch day one: it must accrue. Only then may your reputation precede you. A name is a starting-point of awareness. It is awareness of a name that breeds reputation, not the name itself. Even for an established 'name', reputation needs to be substantiated daily. A name in isolation is an empty vessel. It gathers weight of importance from the fraternity of the other elements it must mix with. A snowflake becomes a snowball becomes the snowman. And it can melt away just as easily through neglect or changes in environment, fashion or attitude. Names can be faddish, suddenly bursting into fashion, departing with a bang or whimper or reappearing from another age as though newly cleaned. Words, through usage, often beyond control, can significantly alter in inference, sometimes being involuntarily rendered unfit for their original purpose – on occasion overnight and without warning. There is a certain graveyard in the land of Identity with numerous unworkable names, wrecks of neglect and glorious failures of names. Time may revive some whilst permanently condemning others.

THE PROBLEM WITH NAMES

Rule number one: don't trust them. Never take any name or, for that matter, any descriptive word for granted. Challenge all the names used within your identity and communication materials by interrogating them for meaning, source and relevance.

It is worth considering that names obstruct as well as construct. For example, if someone innocently asks you what it is you do for a living, how do you answer them? What terminology, qualifications or title do you print on your business card? Looking at your job title, where did this title originate? Your convention or that of another? Does it extend or limit your impact? Is it boastful or modest, explanatory or misleading? In short, is it helpful, or of no use at all? All words are suspect. What does a word mean in terms of your identity? What does it add? Who is it meant to impress – you or the client? Often in business it is best to say nothing. Speak when you need to and contemplate what you say, for so often the terminology of others is allowed to 'invade' an identity unchallenged. Beware, for it steals your thought patterns – words are often the building bricks of thought. Change the bricks and the building changes.

All names and terminology should be questioned in terms of what represents fashion and truth (your choice of classic or romantic). And remember consistency. Once you have vetted the names you are to work with, use them consistently in speech and written material. Pay attention to word detail again and again – and again. Do not overuse names but use them sparingly. Too many names to digest at once or overusage of a name can upset the flow of the real message.

Effective communication should lead to the names, not be obstructed by them. Often the audience must struggle to understand what is being said. Boredom, fatigue and insult – do not inflict them on yourself, your team or your audience. Consider whether the terminology within your literature is helpful, accurate and understandable. Understand that a name or description can be viewed as being positive, negative or neutral in message. Is the polarity of your terminology therefore suitable to the messages you are attempting to communicate? And, is it also memorable?

Your audience must be given the opportunity to remember your name. Then they must want to. Think for a moment about the relationship between how well known your name is now, and how well known you would like it to become in the future. Then think about how memorable your name and the presentation of it are for the audience you hope will remember. Memorable names are valuable. Experiment with names in order to gain the maximum advantage from their presentation. But, long or short name, be cautious when reducing, especially if the result is a group of initials, which though possibly memorable may be more faceless than you imagine. If the initials are obviously memorable, you are fortunate, for more usually they represent a dull and commonplace barrier which limits memory recall – although calm, steady and predictable (even if considered uninteresting) may be just the attributes to suit your objectives.

every name should earn its keep

If you are expecting your audience to become familiar with the full names for which the initials stand, beware that you are not demanding too much or making unwise assumptions about their patience or interest. In addition, you need to evaluate the possibility that, should your organisation develop beyond the point where the original meaning of those initials becomes an irrelevance, impediment or embarrassment, you may be faced with either a change of name or else the abandonment of explanation – the origins are demoted to an anecdote of history. The abstract nature of the initials must now stand with only their remaining merits of distinction, character or memorability.

Initials that form an acronym can be extremely effective as long as they don't insult, irritate or in time become rendered counter-productive to your original aims. Over time, whether as a result of your activities or the progression of society and its language as a whole, acronyms can become assimilated into everyday language and adopted as nouns. Yet the benefit of acronyms is that they can convey complex or lengthy messages which would otherwise be too unwieldy to communicate so easily, assuming they are communicated with style and credibility, anything else being the sign of an amateur.

If the name is a group of initials, how commonplace is the first initial? The importance of this becomes obvious when listed alphabetically in a directory. Some characters of the alphabet are more subscribed to than others. You may be surprised to find that even your complete group of initials is also used by another organisation, albeit perhaps in a different market area. The resultant hindrance of communication may be a major obstacle to your prime objectives: for example, if you are a national or global organisation expecting the general public to remember and recognise your initials, those initials had better be unique as well as being memorable, or else budget for a long-haul advertising and public awareness campaign.

But these points do not just apply to initials, for all names can be just as forgettable: witness most people's difficulties remembering the names of those introduced to them on the first meeting.

In general, do not make things more difficult by including in your name any unnecessary words of dubious benefit. Each word should ideally earn its keep. After all, you already, or intend to, invest a good deal of your resources into promoting this name to your audience.

Status

THE IMPORTANCE OF STRUCTURE

A clearly defined visual structure for an identity and its hierarchy of control and command is necessary if your audience is to understand your organisation and how it conducts its operations. This visual structure and its maintenance are understood to be the perceived authority

you need to plan for visual growth

of the identity. It 'says' who owns whom, and indicates the position of each part of your identity within the parent organisation. This organisation may already exist, or it is the organisational framework of the future that you expect your identity will need to conform and adapt to. It is the structure that your identity will grow into. Like planning your garden, you need to plan for visual growth. If you plant a tree in a tight corner, do not be surprised to find that you need to move or fell it before it is fully grown. Alternatively, maybe the garden you are planning will in time need to merge, be taken over, or take over other areas. You need to design with flexibility as well as purpose. This planning of structure is as important for the internal workings of the organisation as it is for your audiences on the outside, for this visual representation of organisation, status and power must be clearly understood. Your visual structure communicates an inescapable sense of direction and order.

Starting a new identity is like dressing for work. Unlikely as it sounds, in your hurry you might end up putting your underpants on over your trousers. Or end up wearing odd socks. Order and sequence, the what goes first, and the who dresses who, is what this visual structure is all about. It is dressing suitably for need and destination.

An organisation can, if it chooses, group its appearances together, so that all operations are displayed the same, and therefore recognised as one collective entity. This does not just apply to those with only a small range of products sold into the one market. It can also apply to larger, more complex organisations serving unconnected markets. The question to ask is whether the repercussions are worth the economy of stretching one identity across multiple markets.

This decision should be based upon the current demands of the audience, unless you are attempting to redefine the market. Meanwhile, strong forces and personalities within an organisation can lead to calls for devolution or takeover between rival divisions and product offerings. However, despite these occasional pressures, the litmus test is how will the market respond? Will it share your motivation and reward you accordingly, or be confused, nonplussed or alienated by the identity structure you present it with?

The visual system and hierarchy of your identity is one of the main underlying patterns by which your audience will learn to trust you, your apparent values, authority, distribution, ownership and – should you have any – parent organisations, subsidiaries and divisions, and product families.

The larger your organisation's activities, the more vital it is that you pay close attention to a properly considered structure. Too frequently, an otherwise well-organised identity is made prematurely redundant. An expanding business can quickly lose visual clarity, as organisational growth starts to overtake the suitability and flexibility of its visual identity system. It may be a simple case of an expanding range of colour-coded products running out of suitably different colourways, or it might be subdividing divisions entangling themselves in the eyes of your audience and those that work within different product areas. It might be a case of the parent company's identity being too overbearing for the young offshoot now threatening to take over in market importance. Perhaps the parent company's identity needs to be nondescript, or vice versa.

an expanding business can quickly lose visual clarity

A structure begins from the name of the organisation, the names of its subsidiaries, divisions, product ranges and so on. Even the hierarchy of terminology and the necessary levels of documentation can get out of step. The visual linkages between these need consideration, and before it is likely to be a confusing and expensive problem to resolve. Each has a relationship to be negotiated by the identity. There are differing levels – simple-to-know hierarchical issues that your audience will need if they are to navigate your appearance with ease. Some elements need to be publicised more assertively than others. Some elements may need to endorse others, and some deny or have the need to compete with each other. Some elements may need to remain obscure or anonymous. Like any family tree, the centralised or decentralised relationship between these activities and their names dictates the most suitable structure of identity.

In order to proceed you have a choice. There are two clearly defined structures of identity: a Mono-identity or a Multi-identity. Between these two exists a grey area, largely extended and managed by endorsement, or left to grow wild, in which case the notion of structure is lost altogether.

THE MONO-IDENTITY

This is a single visual style for an organisation: one which permeates all its operations and products. A Mono-identity punches its full weight in a single direction, for every element within the identity – and therefore the entire organisation – is clearly seen to support the whole. There is no conflict or competition of values because the structure of the identity speaks with one centralised voice. Because of its apparent simplicity, it seems to be the easiest and most economical structure to manage, but it requires a clarity and discipline few are equipped to maintain.

This category of identity structure can be extended to subsidiaries, divisions and products, but only within the boundaries of remaining a single and clearly understood verification of the central identity. It must still be seen as a totality, even though some relaxation or addition of style may be authorised for semi-autonomous or independent subsidiaries or marketing operations. These fringes mark the beginnings of weakness, for the immaculate hallmark of a Mono-identity is its implicit authority, made possible by its continuous and regulated visual discipline and procedure. It advertises single ownership.

know from the outset whether you will be mono or multi

193

Illustration 26

The Mono-identity

This is a single name and visual style, one which permeates all the products
and operations of an organisation.

Parent
organisation

Subsidiaries
or Divisions

Products
and Services

Illustration 27

The Multi-identity

This is a collection of different names and visual styles applied to different aspects
of the organisation, its products and services.

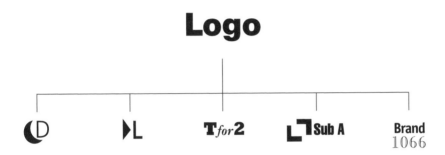

If these same logos are rearranged, this time without the lines denoting the family tree, there is
no longer any clue to their relationship.

THE MULTI-IDENTITY

As the name implies, this is the coexistence of more than one identity. It is often suitable for fast-moving or transient operations where it is useful for the identity of the product to remain autonomous from the parent organisation. Alternatively it may be a result of acquisition, perhaps several companies operating in different sectors – sometimes competitors under the same ownership – all of which enjoy a status and goodwill derived from their existing identities and can see no added value in relinquishing them. They may or may not link to one another by endorsement. The strength with which these differing identities bind together can vary widely. Different divisions or products may appear to be related or unrelated according to whatever degree of closeness suits their current or long-term objectives.

One way of looking at this is to imagine a Multi-identity as the hull of an ocean liner designed with several bulkheads or compartments. Each compartment can appear self-sufficient, should it choose. Dependent upon the level of this interaction or apparent freedom is the risk management of fashion changes, market adventure and failure because, if one bulkhead fails, the effect need not necessarily flood or damage its neighbours. The ship of the organisation should remain afloat, its overall objectives unimpeded. The success of one identity need not be connected with the failure of another. The other benefit of this approach is catering for multiple or fast-moving markets in a manner considered unsuitable or impossible for the parent organisation to be involved in.

The benefit and cost of this independence is a dilution of the perceived overall scale of an organisation's operations. The focus and return of resources diverge: the audience of one sector may remain unaware of the links of ownership (and therefore the possible connection of values) between the main identity of each individual identity. This may be useful to you, depending on the organisation's overriding market need to display bulk. The size of a Multi-identity organisation is difficult for your audience to estimate, except where deliberately publicised, such as a publicly-owned company explaining its trading operation in an annual report, or a pressure group attempting to discredit your operations by revealing trading links you would rather not own up to. The idea is to play structure to achieve benefit. Design structure for productivity. An organisation may deliberately set one division in competition with another – a fabricated contest for the audience, the common audience unaware of the relationship between the two.

Each identity within the whole may be founded upon different values. These may remain separate from those of the controlling organisation, and managed through their unique combination of firmwords, with as many subsets as required. This is a decentralised identity structure that can play hide and seek with a variety of diverse and fragmented areas of operation.

CHOOSE AND MAINTAIN

If you are a new operation, the choice may not seem relevant. The initial extent of your activities, products or services may not appear to need any particular awareness of structure. Yet the moment you voluntarily begin to expand your operations – or the demand is placed upon you to do so – the strains of visual confusion caused by a lack of coordination appear. So it pays to be aware of both current and anticipated structural demands.

The choice or maintenance of a Multi-identity structure offers flexibility and the comfort of marketing experimentation, with no loss of face should not all proceed as planned. It may be considered worth developing a distinct individualistic identity for each market with less regard for the temporary or permanent nature of the opportunity each market presents. If so, a Multi-identity offers a changeable and selective visual umbrella of support; individual products can be endorsed or denied at will by the reputation, name and identity of the parent organisation or brand. As a result, there may be several identities to be developed, maintained and trusted by several audiences. The complexities of this obviously demand a corresponding effort and allocation of resources – it costs money.

Alternatively, the structure of a Mono-identity offers a fixed visual roof to cover all aspects of your activities. Here, each product is endorsed by the reputation, name and identity of the parent organisation. There is only one identity to be promoted, maintained and trusted. As a result, it has the most forceful power-to-weight ratio of identity in terms of the trade-off between effort and reward. The downside for some is that it relies on total concentration, for should any component of the identity suffer, it is the entire identity that pays the price.

You might choose both. Often an organisation suddenly needs to combine the two structures, maintaining a mono approach for its key identity whilst promoting a set of unconnected multiple identities elsewhere.

Illustration 28

A Mono-identity extended over too contradictory a range of market activities.

A Mono-identity retains its credibility and central authority through the smallest of linkages. These connections can be fragile and susceptible to breakage, mistreatment or abuse. If the growing nature of the organisation it represents is allowed to extend itself over too disparate a range of market activities, and where the existing identity struggles to successfully combine this new market diversity, the identity begins to flounder. A Mono-identity cannot be seen to contradict itself. Beware in case you do not see the contradiction as quickly or clearly as your audience. This is a major danger area for a Mono-identity – the unbridgeable gulf or potential abyss whereupon an identity begins to satisfy itself more than the needs of its audience. It is before you reach this point that the restructuring of the identity or else the curtailment of an over-extended or incongruous mixture of market operations must be addressed.

Illustration 29

Munitions

Pop Radio

Kitchen Appliances

If these three organisations (or divisions of an organisation) insist on sharing the same Mono-identity, it must be because they are placing their own self-importance before the needs of their audiences.

One type of organisation susceptible to this problem is one whose management wishes to move faster than the audience either expects or wishes; and perhaps also too fast for the existing identity to keep up with. Entrepreneurs often build or acquire businesses in such a way, with great success or failure. Their difference is, primarily, that they fully realise their continued success depends on their wits, and probably no one else's. They rely on their instincts being in tune with what may always be a fickle and disparate set of audiences. The personality of the entrepreneur can become inextricably linked to the organisation they represent. Personal identity can become a greater market factor than organisational identity. The risk of failure occurs when they personally leave the organisation they founded, or the value of the subsidiary they are seeking to sell is confused with the value of their personal endorsement. In other words if they sell the subsidiary, the trading operation minus the continuance of their personal identity may represent a significant potential loss.

Mono-identities also fail through the gradual or sudden introduction of disparate, irrelevant or incomprehensible patterns of graphics into the centre of their key areas of identity. A Mono-identity thrives on consistency – and those linkages and the intangible values that underpin them must never be compromised, visually fragmented or dissolved by the use of any unsuitable or contradictory signals. Within this type of structure, a strict control of visual focus is essential. Also, if the management fails to understand the identity structure they are operating within, the identity is out of control. The audience may instinctively realise that the identity is losing form, discipline and focus. Furthermore, they may interpret this deviation as a form of devolution; a weakening of the centre. In this way the structural authority of the identity has been challenged, if not set on another course altogether, and previous patterns of expectation altered. It is probable that investors puzzled by a trading difference may not necessarily connect this event with the deviation of the identity. Yet such deviations signal tidal changes of perception, and it is a mistake to imagine that these do not translate into physical gains and losses. If you are measuring the focal values of your show, tell and do you may be able to audit the difference more intelligently, and learn accordingly.

Logos

THE MAGIC OF THE CORRECT LOGO

Ironically, despite the simplicity of the best logos, the more successful they become, the more they may defy conscious recognition. If you doubt this, attempt to draw some famous logos familiar to you, but without any reference. Unless you are exceedingly visually intelligent, you may be surprised at how difficult this task is. Yet even if you fail to visualise the detail of these logos, when you next see them you will, of course, recall them in a flash. What you recall is a certain instant, and it is at this point that the logo is doing its job as both representative and endorser for the other information which may surround it. It acts as a conduit for the rest of the identity.

a logo should play upon the unconscious mind

The best logos play upon the unconscious mind. This is the ideal. However, logos often achieve much less, confusing or thwarting both the viewer and wearer. Some demand too much conscious attention, the viewer becoming distracted by their construction or the significance of meaning. Often, there is not enough quality to match or penetrate the imagination of the viewer. Attention can easily stumble or halt altogether with the logo alone through its failure to lead the viewer beyond itself. A logo should that it represents something of significance and interest, a direction or subject worth following, something more than the sum of itself. If the logo fails to endorse anything beyond or fails to introduce you to a wider sense of identity, its mission is weak, if not futile. This is why an effective identity cannot just rely upon a logo and nothing else. Equally, a logo should never 'give it all away' on first meeting by furnishing too much detail – trying to convey more information than it should be expected to indicate. It is a virtuous element that should rightly refuse to gratify too much too soon. It exists to signpost: it is the signal placed to beckon the viewer to think or believe beyond their current situation.

A bad logo is one which appears lifeless or exhausted. It either tries too hard or fails to try enough. It is ill conceived and uncoordinated, inept for the method of reproduction, the wrong size, inappropriate colour, typeface and message; no logo at all may for many organisations be an improvement.

the best logos are often the ones you take for granted

A logo should promote with clarity the correct values. It is no good getting attention for the wrong reasons or misleading the viewer by promising one thing, yet delivering another. It should promise the truth, or else it might fail through being 'found out'. Like any other aspect of an identity, it must adhere to the correct values of the product or organisation – the firmwords that propel the identity.

ARE YOU SURE YOU NEED A LOGO?

As this chapter explains, there are different variants of logos. This is not argued merely as an academic exercise, but to demonstrate that different variants offer different limitations and opportunities of commercial operation. Even before the design itself can be decided, your choice of logo variant will exert a vital influence over your progress.

There is a temptation to design the logo before anything else. Yet if you feel tempted to rush into this without having examined your firmwords, how will you know if you are exploring the most rewarding areas of design? Instead you are better advised to ask why you should want a logo at all – and if you already have one, why you want to change it. It is best not to make assumptions before leaping into action, and you should never allow your designers to stumble into design before knowing your strategy and firmwords.

For some this is frustrating, but the answer to these critics (and you will have them) is that it is worse to waste energy without direction. Once you have a clear understanding of your requirements, you can decide the correct classification of logo that best suits these objectives and then concentrate your design resources towards those specific aims.

In simple terms you have a name if you wish to be identified. To communicate this name involves tell and show: it must be used orally and must almost certainly appear on visual display material. The manner in which you are seen is therefore the manner in which you will also be judged.

By design or default, an organisation must present its name in a given style, and if it wishes to regulate this and, with deliberation, add further communication to its presentation, it must design and control this sequence of procedure. Through the use of particular typefaces or graphics a name elevates itself to a logo.

Through modern usage, the word 'logo' has come to mean a symbol, a name set in a distinctive typographical style, or a combination of both. A logo communicates with intent to stir emotion, which it should do with a simple ease – simply notable, simply understandable – and, for ease of reproduction, simply reproducible. Make certain your logo will reduce to the smallest reproduction size you require, and maintain its reproduction qualities.

A logo represents. The best provide potent and immediate communication in order to gain recognition, promote a particular set of values and act as endorsement for the bearer.

ENDORSEMENT BY LOGO

Another role of a logo is to endorse the correct values of all the other messages, written or graphic, which surround it. The logo is a central point around which all other messages must be fastened. Ultimately, the act of endorsing is its prime task, the role it will live or die by.

In terms of your identity, think about who is endorsing whom, what is endorsing what? An identity is the interface between physical reality and emotional reality: what is and what is presented. The logo needs to endorse all within this dimension. But what dimension is this exactly? Has anyone bothered to map out its territory? You should do, for the law of this area of operation will be the structure of the identity, the method of interface to be employed – Mono-identity or Multi-identity, as discussed in the previous chapter. These choices are to be made before a designer can fruitfully be given the task of designing the logo itself. Before a logo can achieve anything beyond the confines of the organisation, it must address and endorse the law internally. The type and method of endorsements used must match the type and method of the identity structure best suited to the objectives of the organisation. Planning this structure beforehand saves remedial work later. To reconstruct a logo after the initial launch is an expensive and inconvenient exercise. While the reconstruction work gets under way, the strength of the identity is temporarily weakened – the castle walls can be breached and the progress of the organisation delayed.

It cannot be emphasised enough that an identity requires the capability to grow, change or alter to suit the climate it must survive within.

Firstly, your logo endorses you. Secondly, it endorses your values in accordance with your firmwords. Thirdly, it provides the mechanism for endorsing and communicating the nature of your organisation – centralised or decentralised, subsidiary, product, service or any other activity – internally and externally.

CHOOSE THE RIGHT LOGO VARIATION

Are you using the correct category of logo for your identity? This depends upon your definition of the word 'logo'. Like many words connected to identity, it is not used with enough thought. A 'logo' means only an emblem or device used as the badge of an organisation in display material – in other words, a symbol. Yet there are a number of logo variations, differences which are seldom noted, but differences nonetheless which have wide-ranging implications through the restrictions and opportunities they offer.

The answer may be that a symbol in addition to your name may be the last thing you need. The logo variant correct for you depends upon a number of factors, but certainly you should not rush into any early assumptions about what you believe you need until you have planned your identity structure.

Logos can be broadly classified as two main variants:

- **Logotype** – a name in a particular typestyle
- **Symbol** – a badge or emblem.

In addition there are three others:

- **Combined** – a combined logotype and symbol
- **Integral** – an integrated logotype and symbol
- **Virtual** – a virtual logo, or icon.

THE LOGOTYPE

A logotype is a grouping of initials, a word or group of words which together form a name. It becomes a logotype, with a status beyond simply a name, when it is seen to be consistently used in a defined typeface, either a standard or customised font. It can often be plain in appearance, though the typeface may be the subject of some additional graphic treatment, the objective being to add to or accentuate the meaning or implied value of the name. Another technique is to partially, or entirely, frame the name with a border design intended to strengthen its appearance and defendable space.

A logotype is self-contained in so far as it is capable of use without the need for any other separate symbol or device.

Those three examples depict a plain logotype with no decoration, a logotype with some simple graphic treatment and, finally, a logotype (in this example, plain) with a border device. Any graphics added to a logotype should conform to, and certainly not contradict, the values of the firmwords selected for the identity.

Logotypes are potent when the name or names they contain also have potency. If your name is already understood to be synonymous with the qualities you wish to promote, or is already significantly established in the minds of your audience – or promises to be so – you probably require the simplicity and understatement of a logotype.

Some benefits of a logotype include the following:

- A logotype is simple to execute.

- Logotypes can be more readily designed to appear understated, inferring a certain self-worth and confidence. For those assuming a royal or personal status, you may even want to avoid any display font whatsoever – the inference being that anyone who needs to know knows already: ideal for social climbers and polite personal letter headings. This attitude goes with never printing your name under your signature on a letter: if you are that important, why double the emphasis or show off more than you need to?

- A logotype concentrates attention upon the value of the name itself. This is best if the values of the name are obviously well known, such as an already famous brand or a name intended to be publicised as pretending to be so.

- A logotype is suitable if the character of the name is more pertinent or memorable than any worthwhile symbol could improve upon, given the circumstances – indeed, it might be the case that any additional symbolism would weaken the status of the name.

▌ A logotype is ideal if you are so heavily endorsed by another, or others – Royal Warrant, parent company or group, strength of location, personality, celebrity or other company or product – that a plain logotype is the option least likely to interfere with any other graphics which must surround you.

▌ For reasons of dignity choose a logotype: if symbolism appears to 'try too hard', or is suggestive of poor taste. You may not choose to advertise what you would rather wish to remain private or exclusive; for example, an elite club may not want to be seen beyond its limited target audience. The potential low-key nature of a logotype can be a deliberate camouflage.

▌ If name alone is the most vital ingredient to your marketing efforts, for example the www or any other information directory.

▌ If the name is a brand or subsidiary of a larger group endorsed by another symbol – a situation where more than one symbol would be inappropriate.

▌ Where clarity of message is urgent: a legal instruction or process of law, or perhaps a foreign name where there is a need to spell it out in full. A clever logotype design is an opportunity to benefit from the otherwise difficult spelling or pronunciation of a name by concentrating attention upon it.

▌ For a personal or family name. Or the name of a personality whose character benefits from a direct or simple approach.

▌ If you cannot think of anything else, either because it is not necessary to compete with others, or you haven't the ability or budget to do anything else well enough.

All identities must generally include a logotype, for the name always needs communication. Whether you also require a symbol depends upon the nature of your name, as well as your organisation, audience, values and structure of identity.

Beyond the simple treatment of type, a logotype can be decorated with other graphics. The purpose of this decoration must be to invent something unique: first by choice or invention of typeface, secondly by suggestion or accentuation of intangibles or a message within the name. This may be achieved by transforming one or more of the characters, or adding other non-type-specific elements, such as a border, rules, shape, illustration or other symbolism.

The most common solutions contain these graphics as an integral part of the logotype. However, if the graphics become a symbol separate from the logotype, you need to consider whether they should always be combined with the logotype – in other words, working as a fixed unit or a symbol capable of working independently.

Using both a logo (symbol) and logotype together has its benefits, especially for those who need to control a large, complex organisation; however, if your name constitutes a valuable asset, why distract or divert attention away from it with the addition of a separate symbol? It may be useful to have the two devices, but think this through carefully. The meaning and reason behind employing them, and the demarcation and system of usage, must produce a tangible benefit, or else it may weaken your identity by diverting attention away from the inherent status of the name.

THE SYMBOL

A symbol is a badge that does not include a name. It is designed to stand alone or, on occasion, combine with an otherwise separate logotype. Because it contains no meaningful wordage, its effectiveness to communicate is dependent upon how recognisable it is to the intended audience. Often a symbol may have formerly been combined with a logotype but through common usage, or notoriety, became capable of communicating effectively without the need for the actual logotype to be included. Recognising the symbol implies a common understanding, or even membership, for, with no name, its fame or obscurity may suit its purpose – perhaps the badge of a local club, an entire nation. A symbol is capable of promoting the privacy or exclusivity of its membership. Elect to use a symbol with care in case it appears to an audience as a signal of vanity; many organisations crave a symbol when in fact they do not require one. This is a common failure of identity.

Symbols work best for large operations, especially product-based businesses whose common presence of branded physical products constitutes the main visual manifestation of the organisation: for example, an automobile manufacturer or a company whose consistency of delivery, service or output alludes to being that of a virtual product – such as the inherent and often branded attitude or methods adopted by some institutions which also enjoy an element of personal membership. This includes schools, political movements, fund-raising charities, clubs or other networks or areas of operation. A symbol, being a message for the initiated, works in sectors with limited display areas such as fashion clothing and other articles of decoration where the subtlety of a symbol without name promotes a partnership between the communicator and the audience recognising it. To do this successfully, the symbol must be simple enough to work with printing techniques and have an aspect ratio capable of severe reduction in size – as an extreme example, if used as a decoration on a cufflink.

These three sample logos depict a series of symbols. The first contains the initial 'L' but in such an abstract way it is not necessarily recognisable as such.

A symbol is useful because:

■ It uses no written language and therefore requires no translation.

■ In theory, it is capable of severe size reduction – often beyond the potential of a logotype.

- It can remain identifiable from a greater distance, whereas a logotype at the same distance may be more difficult to 'read'.

- It can be quickly recognised – making it ideal for mass markets.

- It can readily be used to endorse another organisation or product logo, often with no need for any additional logotype.

Symbols mirror the history of mankind. The opportunities to create a truly original design are limited. Though you should attempt to have a more optimistic attitude than this, you must remain vigilant in case the symbolism you use either clashes, offends or has had its meaning hijacked by association with an existing or historical movement, organisation, region, shape, pattern or colour.

THE COMBINED LOGO

A logo can take the form of a combined logo: a symbol and logotype as two separate items but positioned together in order to form a single working unit.

In a combined logo the symbol tends to act as an endorsement of the logotype – perhaps a sign of guarantee or mark of true or pretended prestige. As with all graphics that form part of any logo, the meaning can be literal, suggestive or even purely decorative, but it must always be in tune with the firmwords of the identity.

A combined logo is useful when:

- A logotype is in need of more suggested prestige.

- A name has, or pretends to, a history.

- Different logotypes need to be endorsed by the same symbol.

An example of a combined logo:

A combined logo can be employed to endorse another organisation or (as in this example, with an optional change of colour) the logotype of a product:

THE INTEGRAL LOGO

An integral logo is a symbol which contains a logotype within its own boundaries, as the example below shows.

This has all of the attributes of being a symbol, yet also contains the name. This form of logo is a highly effective medium where certain benefits of using a symbol are most relevant to your needs but you also wish to use the name because it has a quality or value of communication worthy of retention at all times.

The name should ideally be generic enough to work more or less regardless of differences in language and culture. It is also helpful if that name is short enough for the purposes of the symbol to remain effective when being reduced to a small size.

An integral logo is useful when:

▮ The name has some merit but requires added strength.

▮ There is the need for greater opportunity or application of graphics (beyond the possibilities offered within just the logotype).

▮ Small size reproduction is important.

▮ A logo as a badge has obvious uses.

▮ You are endorsing another organisation or product logo.

An integral logo can be employed (with a varying degree of prominence) to endorse another product or (as in this example) the logotype of another organisation:

THE VIRTUAL LOGO

A virtual logo occurs when a product ultimately becomes so established within the broader realms of society that it becomes in effect an icon in its own right. In other words, though possibly badged, the product has little need for the application of a logo. The product is self-defining and self-sustaining, exercising more power than the original pretend brand. It has become a real brand.

This is not necessarily a rare destiny. If the product has enough reputation to stand alone and be instantly recognised, it can be used as a virtual logo – it may supersede the need for the logo because its photographic image at the base of an advertisement substitutes. In this way it can act as a 'sign-off', pretending to 'say it all', especially when combined with a supporting qualification.

The Original. Since 1963.

RELATIONSHIPS

These different logo variants show you how the need to endorse and the mechanics of doing so decide the identity structure and correct choice of logo variant. All these elements need to cooperate or an identity becomes confusing, if not ultimately lawless.

Beyond these elements are the relationships which further assist in explaining the nature of the organisation or product being identified: the relationships between the different components of an identity. These relationships are visual signals which explain who owns, endorses, befriends or authorises whom: a holding company may need to display its relationship with a subsidiary, an organisation with a product, and one brand with another.

PARENT AND CHILD

One way of managing these relationships is to see them as parent and child relationships. A parent may choose to display its relationship between itself and its offspring. The level of dominance or control the parent is seen to exercise over the child can vary. This is where the logo variant of the parent organisation becomes critical. It dictates the boundaries within which the relationship can be visually managed.

 **Subsidiary**–A    **Product**–A

An integrated or symbol parent logo adapts very easily, as the above two examples show.

However, a logotype or combined parent logo where the design does not lend itself easily to being split into separate symbol and logotype (for example, the symbol is so commonplace a graphic as to be rendered meaningless without the logotype supporting it) poses a different set of problems, as shown below.

Logotype

Here, the parent logo, willingly or otherwise, tends to compete with the child, unless countered by differences in scale between the two, which makes the suggested relationship obvious to the audience.

Matters can be clarified by the addition of other explanations.

But the addition of two apparently unrelated logos plants confusion and indicates a nervous parent or child.

If the two logos are seen to be equal, they enter the consenting adult category.

Logotype   **Logo**type

The partnership between the two logos may not be clear unless explained. Are they together by choice or not? Are they equals which together form one unit – such as a consortium? You may insist that you are equals, yet cynical audiences will always seek to guess which is the dominant partner. Such relationships need to be handled with great sensitivity.

If the relationship is more specific, again you will need to qualify the partnership.

In general, the public approval or endorsement between a parent and child works in both directions. A child can benefit from the status or heritage of its parent, sharing the reputation of the parent where the audit trail or genealogy is both useful and appealing to the target audience.

QUALIFICATIONS

A logo is a form of self-qualification. You have branded yourself, and this logo advertises you both in person and in your absence.

In addition to the relationships of any parent organisation or affiliated brand exists the management of other self-awarded qualifications and selling points such as location, age and other explanations, temporary or semi-permanent badges or supporting lines of text. Also the licence, endorsement or other seal of approval by an independent source may qualify you.

Geography

 • LONDON

Age

 • ESTABLISHED 1835

Subject or product area

 • MENSWEAR

Values or call to action

 • JOIN THE NETWORK NOW

Personality

 • AS WORN BY *Lowe*

Point of contact

 • TELEPHONE 123 4567 8900

Logos are not limited to having only one type of relationship or qualification – they can be mixed and matched in order to suit your purpose and audience, as the following examples show:

 • GO ON… SAY IT… www.firmwords.com

[ROYAL SEAL] • OF BOND STREET

 • UK • ENGINEERING

 • of England • ENGINEERING

 • of England • FROM 1902

NEW  • RELIEF FROM HEADACHES

 • MATURE CHEDDAR • TASTE THE DIFFERENCE

Trust  • *to always get it right!*

 • LONDON – PARIS – ROME

 • 24 HOURS • www.firmwords.com

Welcome to  *WORLD*

Qualifications act as both limitations and advantages. Establish them with care, giving clear instructions for their integration with your logo. Enshrine these instructions as a clearly explained part of your identity guidelines. Specify typefaces, sizes and positioning details so as to ensure a uniform appearance. If you fail to make the rules clear, these 'add-on' elements will look just that: random and ill-considered, reducing the effectiveness and authority of your logo. Any additional elements which appear alongside your logo should be marshalled to appear as a deliberate and fully intended, authorised integral statement.

In the area of audiovisual communications, these qualifications may be delivered orally or by animation, but of course they still form part of your identity. So, again, care must be taken for the sake of consistency and integrity.

You should try to recognise the expected lifespan of the qualifications you intend to use – some may match the lifespan of the identity, but most will fade through use over a shorter period. Distinguishing the timeless from the transient is a key element of qualification management. Beware, for what you may judge today as being permanent or transient may tomorrow suddenly veer in the opposite direction. An additional phrase can become more notable than the rest of the identity, perhaps a catchphrase – for better or worse. Alternatively, and sometimes overnight, it can become your worst nightmare.

Any qualification or relationship between your identity and logo and another more temporary element can over time marginalise the identity, rendering it entrenched with a set of values you may not have anticipated or planned for. An identity can so easily get stuck because of its associations and qualifications. Likewise, published statements of policy and opinion or the associations with the newly famous or infamous can quickly overtake you. For example, a scandal breaks about a personality paid to endorse you, or something you say about yourself, even a casual aside, suddenly comes, through the connivance of fate, to appear dangerously negative. If you recognise marginalisation too late, the qualification may trap and seal the fate of your identity.

It is not uncommon for a qualification to hijack an identity. For example, a startlingly successful phrase or memorable jingle might overtake you. Treat additional qualifications like the 'extras' you add to a production to make it more spectacular, attractive or believable. If you manage them like this then you will not go wrong. The trouble arises when an extra shines brilliantly beyond its original support role and then starts to steal the show. To begin with this extra impact and attention may be welcomed, but over time it may gradually sidetrack the other things you would, by then, rather be saying – like a veteran artist wishing to perform new tunes with an audience that won't let them escape the success of their former hits.

So, before the beneficial effect of a qualification assumes too much permanence, it is prudent to introduce a replacement qualification to maintain the mobility of the identity. If you do not react in time, it becomes increasingly difficult to make the change. And do realise that change is likely to be necessary before the point when the audience decides to tell you.

Arrivals

DEPARTING TO ARRIVE

A new identity is a departure. It is a launch pad for the new and a break with the tradition of yesterday for those changing direction, however marginal or revolutionary.

As with any strategy, departure points involve risk. Introducing the new requires the coordination of the product and distribution that this identity is seeking to promote and assist. It is nothing less than the management of expectations. If it is a relaunch, however far you are breaking with the expectations of the past, or rushing to meet the expectations of the future, it is unlikely to be a complete divorce from the old identity, for traces of history tend to remain. This is not just in the short term, whilst the new identity establishes a beachhead, but in the longer-term memories and attitudes of those who will now live with and observe the changes you are subjecting them to. If a supplier of yours changes their identity, one of your first reactions might be: why? Why are they doing this, and how does this profit me? Does it represent a valuable set of new expectations? In other words, are they increasing their benefits to me, or maybe seeking to diminish them? For example, if a credit card changes name, does this also signify a change of ownership and terms and conditions? Change is disruption: it bolsters confidence or introduces new insecurities.

audiences need to be led from one stability to another

That is why it might require clear and pertinent explanation. Your identity change may take your audience off-guard. There may also be practical issues to promptly address: a change of name means customers and suppliers may be subject to legal agreements being rewritten.

Audiences need to be led from one stability to another. You are about to lead them in the direction of *your* choosing. Some will complain of the inconvenience, but this doesn't mean they will not follow. The art is to allow only those casualties you intend. This period is also an opportunity to quietly redefine your customer and supplier base. A new identity is a new focus of mentality, and as such will refocus your audiences. Take advantage of the changeover to adjust other commercial and financial changes as necessary. The realignment of your new identity internally and externally means all relationships are perceived to be travelling through a state of change anyway, so make the changes go as deep as you need, and work them in tandem to the new identity. If your identity is as integrated with your strategies of product and distribution as it should be, the structural changes this identity presents will correspond to reality. A new visual structure translates to a new physical structure. A new policy on terminology might as well translate to a new definition of divisional boundaries and job titles as well as anything else. Changes in identity should translate to real changes, or else why do it? The virtual changes that so many identities have delivered to us in the past have left many of us jaded. No wonder many laugh at yet another organisation changing its name to no tangible effect. Instead, the intentions should be clear: you change your name, as with any other change, for a clearly understood and profitable purpose. Refining or changing identity should be about changing alignment and trajectory.

At what speed you dispense with the past and usher in the new will depend on many factors. For many, with product in the field, the new identity will have no alternative but to operate alongside the old. This is not the problem it may seem to some, for if the old identity has any value at all, there will no doubt be some sympathy shown towards it within the new design. However, if the old product is an embarrassment, then make sure the new identity disowns it. For small and medium-sized organisations the phasing in of the new identity may be undertaken quickly and with the minimum of fuss, or – in certain situations – with only partial announcement. Announce to your critical audience if only over lunch, and warn all those whose surprise may be important to you. Some customers might silently think you are refocusing your business away from them. They might fear that your advance or growth is a threat to them, and if you fail to politely explain your actions may take these changes as a signal to trade elsewhere. Changes of stealth have their advantages and economies of action, but they cause shockwaves.

A large organisation changing its identity will by necessity need to introduce publicly and with a full explanation. Due to the extent of identity in the field, such as a large network of stores or depots, these changes may need to be introduced step by step, because often the physical changeover is not possible any other way. Depending upon the complexity of the organisation's operations, and its number of audiences, a series of programmes may need to be launched – some, but not all, simultaneously – from the basic principles for stationery, sales promotion, literature, packaging and product identification to architectural, vehicle or transport identification, and so on. There may also be a need for publications or events to inform the rest of the organisation about the behavioural changes and ongoing progress of implementation well after the initial launch.

Large or small organisation, you need to be expedient in the running down of old supplies. Group your actions and conduct as few stages of changeover as possible. Whatever you do there will be some wastage but the profitable effect of the new identity will quickly compensate. If by this late stage this worries you, then it is a sign that things are very wrong.

Last is often first. Or second can overtake first. Followers can become leaders. The rush to get under way can be extreme. Impatience on the start line gives rise to nerves and pressure. Yet most pressure is self-inflicted. You create it, expect it, or even demand it. There will always be a reason for travelling faster or getting there first. After all, you can see the benefits of the new identity before others. In your mind it exists already. The temptation not to hold back until a proper launch can be fully stage-managed is, for some, impossible to resist. The very process of creating identity creates pressure. Implementing and then launching tends to add to this sense of urgency. A launch date must be set which allows you to accommodate the necessary preparation and

last is often first

planning, and then you simply must work to it. Do not pre-emptively launch forwards and dissipate your energies by starting before the starter drops his flag. Likewise do not stall on the grid and miss the start of the race.

Before the new launch, sundry renewals or stationery reprint requirements will inconveniently make demands on you. It is wise not to let the interruption of such relatively minor demands upset your planning. Keep a cool head. If necessary, prior to the official launch date, make whatever reissues necessary. Or, confront the fear of not responding – instead, make do without – it may be better! Keep the larger picture in mind rather than the pettiness of minor economics. The long-term worth of your identity should be far more valuable than any temporary shortfall of your current presentation or print stocks.

A launch is an announcement. Public or private, full dress or casual, the function awaits you. A definite launch event is useful because it collects and concentrates the mind, bringing the culmination of your work to an inescapable deadline. The identity, its hopes and fears, and those responsible for them, will be judged anew from the moment of the announcement. Speaking to a wide public or external audience is now a different matter compared to dwelling upon the same issues within the theoretically private walls of the steering group or wider organisation. The external pressures may be more irrational and destructive than the internal pressures experienced so far, but they complete the cylindrical process of criticism. By taking an identity to market you are declaring your readiness and quality of workmanship and management. Do not be swayed by external criticism at this stage. Your launch is still in critical phase, and you must now see it through. The time for evaluation is before or after a launch, not during the middle of one.

keep the larger picture in mind rather than the pettiness of economics

The announcement of a new organisation differs from the re-identification of an existing organisation. There are also takeovers, where a new identity needs to be an adaptation, blend or complete submission to another existing identity. There are other issues to address when changing name, occupation, market or category focus. There are product launches within the safer domain of an already successful corporate identity or related to a family of already established products. The full extent of these permutations and the risks they pose seem endless.

The correct protocol or convenient pecking order for the identity's communication is a matter of manners and politics. Immediately prior to launch, good management suggests that it is wise to think internally first, externally second. Politics and manners decides whether and in which order you include investors, staff, customers, prospective customers, suppliers, agencies, press and media.

There is no substitute for thoroughness except chaos. Launching to these different audiences gives you three basic choices of attitude: talking down, up, or equal to equal. Whatever your decision, take care not to offend or upset the feelings of anyone more than necessary. Schedule in detail, coordinating the various elements and programme of events with patience and thoroughness.

GUIDANCE

A sense of order is a basic requirement of any identity. To achieve this through design there needs to be an acknowledgement and adherence to a number of rules. A clear explanation of these laws to others is necessary if they are to both understand and then successfully follow. Without clearly stated laws and guidelines an identity cannot be effectively managed.

Most of those who need to communicate, propagate or be involved in the interpretation of the identity will need to be closely regulated. Many cannot be trusted to behave themselves otherwise. This is understandable. It is most commonly a cause of the inability to know any better, but there may also be factions whose attitude will be hostile, insurgent or obstinate because they wish to empire-build themselves, are jealous or insecure by nature, or else wish to escape what they see as the imposition of a foreign authority. Likewise, these elements may also seek to undermine any inadequacies in the content or presentation of the laws or guidelines themselves. They may believe that if they can disprove or render foolish even the smallest of guidance, they may succeed in undermining or fostering a wider-ranging condemnation of the controlling authority. Of course, any failings brought to the attention of the authors should be received

there is no substitute for thoroughness except chaos

223

graciously, and constructive reportage and fault-finding is to be highly valued, indeed sought after. The issue is one of leadership: the recognition of loyalties and motives, and not overreacting or responding inappropriately, or too soon or too late.

If you tire, you lose. Even though you may state things clearly, there will still be those occasions when others will fail to understand – most probably because they were in a hurry. They may claim that you miss the point, when the point is there for all to see. They may claim that one instruction contradicts another, when, with a little more understanding of the overall intent, they would realise it does not. They may disagree on an item, word or instruction because of their entrapment by another persuasion – previous belief, habit or convention – which you strenuously and intentionally disregard and challenge. Their previous experience or training, though it may have some worthy values, may seek to oppose this new way forward, because it cannot take such a leap of faith as to knock away the foundations of their personal traditions. To return to an earlier chapter, you have identified your position and prepared yourself for attack. The assaults do not disappear after a launch; an identity and its preservation are under continual challenge of attrition.

Meanwhile, and on a more positive note, the more creative members of your team may be expected or invited to make their valued contribution towards the continuing development of the identity. Therefore the guidelines will need to allow a focus around which creative freedom should be welcomed, and provide a framework and procedure within which these contributors can constructively exercise themselves.

*if you tire,
you lose*

In general, too much legislation can be tiresome and unnecessary. It can also be costly, for it involves added time for those whose job is to implement these laws (24 pages or 300 pages, an identity manual needs to be read and understood before any design work can begin). Yet having too few guidelines can lead to abuse of the intended identity through lack of sufficient instruction. This increases the chances of the identity suffering at the hands of others who, caring less than you, simply decide to interpret what rules there are to suit their own convenience. But the opposite, too much complexity, can prove counter-productive if it demotivates those who are required to understand and fully implement. The ideal should be a virtuous circle, where the identity (your identity, their identity) inspires. In this regard, whatever the format of the guidelines, the inspirational nature of the content and its ease of use greatly assist effect and reward.

Where the detail of these guidelines ends, and the ability of management, staff and suppliers takes over, should be a matter of continued debate. This is because, by remaining interested in the aims of the project, you will make certain that the organisation continues to argue, build and maintain an identity which may radiate with clarity, distinction and purpose. Identity development, just like any other facet of an organisation's strategy, should never stand still, or at least not for long.

Distil the points you need to make until you can reduce no more. Even so, the volume of work in covering the necessary areas of instruction is usually fairly extensive. An identity is much more than the simple implementation of a logo. Many will have need to consult the guidelines: from those whose only wish is to create an overhead slide or word-processed document to those responsible for vehicle livery, signage, exhibitions, behavioural training sessions or publicity brochures – all will benefit and thrive from clear instruction, or else have no choice but to produce their own interpretation of the law.

There will be eventualities that cannot be covered by any guidelines, however well planned they may be. You need a communication channel available for those who seek further clarification, and the supply of additional materials. This can be someone internal to the organisation or external, providing, if externally based, they also belong to the original steering committee. This is necessary because continuity and authority is a requirement. The endorsement for this role should be given – and seen to be given – from the very top of the organisation. They should be a representative or ambassador of the organisation's leadership – nothing less. This indicates commitment and the understood ability to enforce the rules as necessary. It signals to all involved that their work or contribution to the working of the identity is both valued and judged by those in the highest authority. Failure to implement this process leads to neglect and carelessness, with the resultant lack of focus. The identity will wander and most likely be abused, unintentionally or otherwise, by those who will soon realise they are operating without enough instruction or feel free from any clear regulation. If the rules can be confused, ignored or overwritten at will, then there is no longer any form of planning permission. Your structure will be in danger because the engineering and maintenance of your identity is subject to a very different form of order – creeping anarchy.

As the process of implementation takes place, issues of loyalty to the new ideal will be important to you. Loyalty for most people is determined by an identity's success. For those who must work with the new guidelines, their effect will soon become apparent. Despite any initial resistance, a noticeable increase in morale should follow. The definition for this success begins only *new is* as a measurement of opinion and faith, but this should *never-ending* soon give way to more tangible measurements – such as increased demand and profitability. In other words, a carefully prepared identity will work wonders for an organisation's progress, if you are willing and patient enough to measure its effect.

For retailers, success or failure of an identity triggers a profit or loss more rapidly than any other areas of business operation. A failing shop with a poor identity, refitted yet selling the same stock, can potentially turn profit to loss with surprising alacrity. In other areas of business activity, the effects of identity and brand can take much longer to become apparent, which is the reason why you must closely manage implementation.

REVISITING

New is never-ending. An organisation needs to be kept informed about the issues that affect its identity. Information should be updated and distributed to those who need to be kept informed.

A launch date also provides an anniversary – and often we may wonder whether we need the reminder of any anniversary, including this one – but such checkpoints are an important time for reflection, celebration or more sober reminder, all of which should help you preserve and maintain a safe and worthy destiny. If you are the creative agency behind the identity maybe a birthday card to a select few would not go amiss. How confidently you send this will speak volumes as to the quality of your original input, as well as serving to remind all those involved that a launch date is no ending, but a beginning.

Consider that the identity launch was a success. Business is booming and you are on your way towards your cherished objectives. You have a firm grip upon the management and ongoing interpretation of the identity. You are able to judge for suitability each design and proposition that you encounter on your road ahead. You understand the visual ingredients, which together constitute your identity at its best. You understand the justification for your use of colour and shape. You are consistent, unbending in your application and authority. The benefits of your identity are compounding daily. The original design continues to improve in scope, demonstrating its intelligent use and benefits. You have entered into and taken the identity to new levels of detail and glory. You are more than ever attentive to the correct and incorrect, and continue to challenge all that you do. The leading edge of your identity is the daily renewal which confirms that your design corresponds to the values of the product and organisation's objectives. The course you originally set is bearing fruit.

you have a choice: to compete or win

Great news, but things change in unforeseen ways. An identity is linked to your product and services, marketing and distribution. People change, events mould us. Technology invents new methods of process and production, demand and abandonment. And so an identity must reassess itself in the light of the current experience, reshaping to the continuing changes thrust on us. The newly important or commonly irritating problems which affect the identity, and which the current strategy and guidelines do not adequately cover, should be acknowledged. If things are wrong and the answers elude you, there should be a process of evaluation and rectification. Guidance must be updated to adapt, or else be rendered obsolete. The management of the identity is in your hands. You made the initial investment – it has been paying you back in return. But that investment cannot and should not be just a one-off. Your identity flourishes or dies according to the ongoing attention you provide it with. It is your partner and friend. Take good care of it if you want it to remain profitably effective and loyal.

FINALLY

You have a choice: to compete or win. The two are different. The former is compliance with a game where team spirit rules. You allow and welcome competition because it is profitable to do so, or because you fail to or choose not to consider the alternative: winning. This is where there is only one focus: your killer instinct for your organisation's victory. Whichever option you choose, the truth is that you are on your own. You are free to determine your own direction, comply with your own guidelines or the guidelines of others, to whatever tolerance of discipline or carelessness. The art of identity is to create that which is, or over time becomes, undeniably you. This living identity begins and ends with you. There is no delegation of responsibility for its understanding and maintenance. You source yourself to propel yourself.

That self, that difference, should you remain determined enough to identify yourself, and continue to develop this truth, is certain to be both unique and powerful. Together with above-average product and/or distribution on your side, your audience will eventually be unable to avoid you, and the rewards of having set your sights on a higher level of integration and performance from your identity will be yours.

Index